CONTENTS

Biddy Baxter, Edward Barnes and **Lewis Bronze**
devised and wrote the **Blue Peter Book**

This edition published by Macmillan Children's Books, by arrangement with BBC Books, a division of BBC Enterprises Ltd.
Blue Peter is a registered trade mark of the British Broadcasting Corporation.

Hello There! from Blue Peter

1

2

3

4

And it's great to be back with the Twenty-Third Blue Peter book! It's packed full of our favourite highlights and like the Blue Peter Review of the Year, it's been a tricky problem to decide what to include and what to leave out.

It's been a year with lots of changes and new developments. Mark took over when Simon became the programme's Countryside Correspondent and Caron joined when Peter went back to the theatre for his Panto and finished off his Duncan Dares filming. Janet achieved her lifetime ambition of creating a new free fall record and you can read all about her record breaking jump on page 16.

A very sad piece of news was that Rags, our pony for disabled riders, became ill and had to be put to sleep. She was 17 years old and had given over 10,000 rides to handicapped people. Goldie's puppy Bonnie became the Blue Peter dog and dear old Jack died in April 1986 – just after a song had been specially composed in his honour. Willow, a beautiful Balinese Varient has taken his place. She doesn't disappear but she's very independent and one of her tricks is exploring the

5

Do you recognise any of these photographs? They've all been on Blue Peter. Turn to page 76 for the answers.

Pete Duncan

PETER

4

ventilation ducts in the studio – rather like a mountaineering rabbit!

Don't miss the stunning photos of Willow and of Bonnie and her brothers and sisters. And there's news of how Buster, Fergie, Honey, Henry, Bonzo, Halley and Snowy are getting on as trainee Guide Dogs for the Blind.

It was also a year in which Blue Peter viewers collected 2,500,000 T-Shirts for the people of war torn Mozambique and Saved the Sight of nearly 2,000,000 men, women and children in Africa. If *you* helped these very good causes, congratulations on what you've achieved. You can catch up with the final results of the Sight Saver Appeal on page 12.

The programme's V.I.P. guests have included Bob Geldof, The Peking Opera, the China National Youth Orchestra, Yasuhiro Yamashita – Japan's Olympic Judo Champion, Jim Henson and Kermit, Burmese – the Queen's horse for the Trooping the Colour ceremony, Chris Amoo and Crufts Supreme Champion – Viscount Grant and Alex and Thomas Parkinson, the 11-year-old twins who trekked through Nepal and climbed 5,486 metres (18,000 feet) – to name but a few.

For the first time ever there's been a Blue Peter Omnibus – a chance to catch up with the week's programmes on Sunday mornings. Lots of people requested this and it's been very popular.

As always, the best ideas for Blue Peter have come from you, the viewers, so please keep on sending them and telling us what you'd like to see every Monday and Thursday. There's a reminder of our address on page 76 and details about the way you can win a Blue Peter badge.

1988 will be the year of Blue Peter's **THIRTIETH** Anniversary, so if you've any suggestions about how we should celebrate – don't forget to let us know!

JANET   x   **MARK**   **CARON**

BONNIE   **WILLOW**   **GEORGE**

5

AVALA

You hear it first. The distant rumbling, like far-off thunder, getting nearer and nearer, echoing down the mountainside. Then you see it, a mighty unstoppable wall of snow, at first moving slowly, then it's crashing, tumbling down, smothering all before it, and leaving a new landscape in its wake . . .

A vital link in the rescue team – Constable Stuart Obree in Glencoe Police Station alerts the helicopter crew.

There's no word which strikes more terror into the heart of an experienced mountaineer. Those that have seen one in real life know there's absolutely nothing you can do to stop one. If you get hit, your only chance is to hope you'll fall into an air pocket so you can survive until rescue comes.

Avalanches are common in Britain's highest mountain ranges, the Cairngorms and the Grampians. Every year they claim a couple of lives, and a few more climbers usually fall victim to other dangers, like exposure and accidents. Of course, the vast majority of people who climb and walk on the hills and mountains have a marvellous time and return home safely. But there are some who get into difficulties and that's when the men and women of the mountain rescue teams are called out from their farms and villages.

Without these dedicated teams, many more people would die. They are led by men like Hamish MacInnes, who runs the Glencoe

Mountain Rescue Team, in the heart of some of Scotland's highest and most rugged mountains. Hamish is the acknowledged world expert on mountain rescue and survival techniques. He's been on *seven* expeditions to the Himalayas alone, and in 1975 conquered the south-west face of Everest. He took me on a walk up Stob Coire nan Lochain, for him no more than the equivalent of a gentle stroll in his back garden. To me, it was tough going, and I slipped and slid along in his wake.

I'd come to see his team in action, not on a real rescue, but on a training exercise, the sort of thing the team has to do to make sure all its different parts, spread half way across Scotland, work together smoothly. That was why a second man, Peter Weir, was with us, and why he and Hamish were carrying spades. Peter was going to be our pretend avalanche victim, and the spades were so he could be buried in the snow.

Peter was fully equipped, with a survival bag, food and two-way radio. Even on a training exercise, it would be extremely foolhardy not to prepare for something to go wrong.

With Peter buried in his snowhole high on the mountain, Hamish put the training rescue exercise into action. He called up the nearest in a chain of listening stations – in this case, a nearby farmhouse.

"Hello, Doris, hello Doris. Avalanche on Stob Coire nan Lochain. Alert the rescue team."

That was the first in a well-rehearsed routine of radio and telephone calls which brings out the team of 20 people. The local police are also alerted and they summon a rescue helicopter from RAF Leuchars, 85 miles from

Glencoe. By the time Hamish and I had struggled down the snowy mountainside, the rescue was in full swing. Hamish's mobile control van had arrived, equipped with all the necessary rescue gear. The people who would make up the search party, were getting a full briefing from Hamish before they set out.

"Avalanche at this grid reference. One climber escaped and raised the alarm. One climber missing on the mountain, assumed buried under snow."

While the search party headed up the mountain, Hamish waited for the next link in the chain, his secret weapon.

"Auric will sort it out," he murmured, while we waited, "He's worth 20 men."

"Who's this superman Auric?" I wondered. And I soon found out – not a man at all but the police avalanche dog, a specially trained

Hamish MacInnes and I climbed up the 1200 metres of Stot Coire Nan Lochain in the heart of the Cairngorms.

NCHE!

tried out the snowhole for size. This is where our pretend
avalanche victim, Peter Weir, was hidden.

**At his Mobile Control Centre, Hamish used his walkie-talkie
to keep in contact with the advance party of rescue climbers.**

Alsatian skilled at sniffing out people under the snow. Auric, his handler Romus Gudelis, Hamish and I all waited while the sounds of the chopper blades got nearer and nearer. Flight Lieutenant Tony Vizard dropped it down close by and we all scrambled in. In seconds, the chopper was airborne again, swinging up towards the snowy slopes of Stob Coire nan Lochain. Hamish got his radio out and called up Peter, who had been buried for over three-quarters of an hour.

"Come in, avalanche victim. Have you eaten your chocolate yet, Peter?"

Back came the crackle over the radio, "Hello Hamish. Yes, it's all gone. Save some food for me." It was clear that Peter was coping well.

From a couple of hundred metres up, we could easily see the hill party plodding up the mountain. They were approaching the spot where we knew Peter was buried, so Tony flew closer, and we prepared to be winched down. Landing was out of the question on the sheer slope. First down was Hamish. Then Auric and his handler, using a special dog harness. Then it was my turn. I've

Going down! Winchman Flight Sergeant Duncan Muir lowered me from the Wessex hovering ten metres above the snowy slopes.

Police avalanche dog Auric dropped in to join the team, in his special harness and held by his handler Romus Gudelis.

7

never been winched out of a helicopter before, and I found it very exciting, although a lot harder than it seems. There's not much you can do, holding on to the end of the cable, and any violent movements to alter your direction will probably result with your body swinging back, even more out of control. The winchman let out the cable, and after a few seconds I felt my feet firmly on the ground once more.

We went on to join the search party. They'd reached the map reference Hamish had given them, and were strung out in a straight line, probing the snow with three-metre long aluminium poles. When their leader gave then command "Forward!", the whole team advanced one pace and started probing again. But they stopped to give Auric the chance to explore the area immediately in front of them.

Auric was panting to get off his lead. He bounded away, sniffing the snow, and moving back and forth across the line of searchers. I was fascinated by his thoroughness, wasting no time on false leads, and giving anything vaguely promising a second sniff before moving on. Auric soon discovered a scent. He started barking and digging in the snow. He had found Peter! The rest of the

The climbers advanced slowly, carefully probing the snow to see if anyone was buried underneath.

search party gathered round and used their shovels and ice axes to extract him.

It was just over an hour since Hamish had made the first emergency call. 15 men had assembled from miles around and, fully equipped, they'd made it up the mountain. The helicopter had arrived from its base on the other side of the mountain range, and had linked up with the police dog and the rescue team. The whole exercise had worked very smoothly – a tribute to planning and organisation, as well as to the bravery of the people who are prepared to put their own lives at

risk to save others. For anyone venturing up to the Highlands of Scotland, it's a comfort to know that Auric, Hamish and people like the Glencoe Mountain Rescue Team are on hand if things go wrong.

P.S. Just after the training exercise ended, the alarm went for real. Tony Vizard's Wessex flew to Ben Nevis, ten miles away and rescued two mountain walkers in distress. All in a day's work!

P.P.S. After our filming Auric won the Police Dog Action of the Year title for saving two climbers trapped on a mountainside.

Once Auric got to work, Peter was quickly rescued. Auric sniffed him out and the climbers cleared the snow to let Peter out of his icy prison. He was very pleased to see us!

PEACH MELBA

When we sailed through Sydney Harbour on our
Expedition to Australia, we couldn't miss this
extraordinary looking building – it looked a bit like a
pterodactyl waiting to swoop over the water! It
turned out to be an Opera House – and people who
only think of Australia as an outdoor, rugged
country full of kangaroos and cricketers forget its
long tradition of opera and great singers.

The first great Australian opera
singer was known all over the
world as 'Melba'. She was born in
Melbourne on May 19th 1861 – but
in those days no one had heard of
Melba – her name was Helen
Porter Mitchell, and she was
called Nellie.

When she was only six years
old, Nellie took part in her first
concert. It was in the local public
hall and it was rather like Saturday
Superstore's Search for a
Superstar! Little Nellie stood on a
chair and sang the old Scottish
song "Comin' Thro' The Rye".

Afterwards she asked another
little girl if she had liked her
singing.

"The singing was alright," she
replied, "but, Nellie Mitchell, *I saw
your drawers!*"

**Helen Porter Mitchell aged 6. After her first concert – a school
friend said, "The singing was alright – but I saw your drawers!"**

9

It must have been a ghastly moment, but nothing stopped Nellie going on with her singing.

When she grew up, she married and had a little boy, but she still wanted to sing more than anything in the world. She gave concerts and was paid £5 a time for them.

When she was twenty four years old, she left Australia to come to Europe, to go to a great singing teacher, called Madame Marchesi.

As soon as she heard Nellie sing, Madame exclaimed,

"At last, I have found a star!" – and Nellie always said "Madame Marchesi is the greatest teacher of them all!"

But stars aren't called 'Nellie Mitchell', so she decided to change her name. Nellie was proud of being Australian and wanted her audiences to remember she came from Australia, so she called herself 'Melba' – after Melbourne, the city where she had been born.

In 1887, Madame Melba sang in an opera house in Europe for the first time. Her career as a great singing star had begun and it lasted for forty years!

Melba appeared in glittering opera houses all over the world. Now her voice was rich and glorious and she gave pleasure wherever she went. Royalty and famous people wanted to meet her; she wore expensive clothes and jewels, and stayed in luxurious hotels.

Once she gave a grand party at London's smart Savoy Hotel. The head cook, the famous chef Escoffier, sent a block of ice carved into the shape of a swan to Melba's table. Between its wings rested a silver bowl, and in the dish was a most delicious pudding.

Melba congratulated the chef, and asked him what it was called.

"I would like to call if after you – *Peach Melba*," he replied.

After sixteen triumphant years, Melba went back to Australia and visited Melbourne. Crowds flocked to meet her, and she was treated like a queen. Now she was paid £2,500 for a concert not just £5 like in the old days.

In 1914 War broke out and Britain and Australia fought side by side. Melba worked tirelessly singing to the troops and raising money for the Red Cross. After the War, she was honoured by being made a Dame of the British Empire. Now she was known as Dame Nellie Melba.

But she was getting older and her voice was not all it had once been. She found it difficult to take

This rare archive photograph shows Nellie Melba making a record at the HMV studios.

The famous chef, Escoffier, created a special pudding in honour of Dame Nellie Melba – Peach Melba!

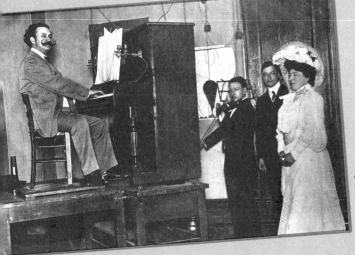

a leading role throughout a long opera, yet she loved to sing as much as ever and she could still manage songs in concerts, so she began to make long tours of many cities, giving farewell concerts.

Sometimes people laughed because she gave so many final farewell performances, but it was because she hated to think that there would be a time when her voice was heard no more.

But that day never came! Melba lived into the Twentieth Century – the recording age, with the invention of the gramophone. She was deeply interested in making recordings, although she

Dame Nellie Melba became an international star – even gramophones and their needles were named after her!

once said to a friend, "Singing for the gramophone was not a rest cure!" Her records reached an audience far larger than the world's opera houses – and she also made a great deal of money from her recordings.

The Melba Horn Gramophone was named after her, and a firm even manufactured Melba gramophone needles – every single needle had Melba's name engraved on it.

Recording equipment in those early days was very primitive, but some of her records still survive. They have been 'restored', so that by a technical miracle we can hear Melba sing today nearly as well as she sang for the great and famous, all those years ago.

There's another way Nellie Melba's remembered, too

'Peach Melba', the delicious pudding that Chef Escoffier made for the great Prima Donna, has been successful ever since and here's a version you can make for yourself! It's a great pudding for a special occasion and the recipe couldn't be more simple:-

Mash up half a pound (250g) of raspberries, tinned, frozen or fresh.

Add 3 or 4 tablespoons of *sifted* icing sugar – and you must sift it first because icing sugar's often quite lumpy.

Put a scoop or slice of ice cream in a pretty dish, add two peach halves (tinned or fresh) and then a spoonful of raspberry sauce over the top.

P.S. If you can't get hold of any raspberries – you can make the sauce with raspberry jam diluted with very hot water and allowed to cool.

SIGHT SAVERS

THE GREAT BLUE PETER BRING AND BUY SALE

You're two years old when one day you feel ill. You've got measles. It happens to thousands of children every year. The doctor comes, you take some medicine, and in a week or so you're running around again, right as rain. But if you were a child in Africa, things might not be so simple. Over there, measles is a serious disease. And every year, millions of children like you become blind, because they've had the measles.

That's what happened to Emmanuel, who lives in a village near Lake Malawi in Central Africa. He caught measles when he was a year old. No antibiotics, no visits from the doctor for him. He went blind. One day he could see, the next day he couldn't, and although he couldn't have known it, all that stretched before him was a long life of being a burden to his family. Being blind, he

The tragedy of eye disease: five year old Ailsa is treated for trachoma. Thousands of children like her go blind due to infections that aren't dealt with quickly.

12

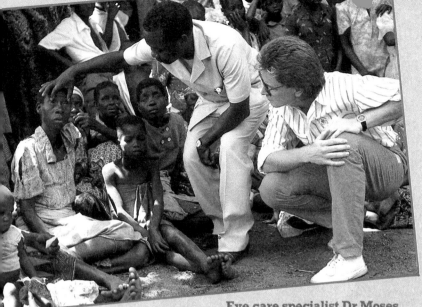

couldn't work in the fields or move to the town to try and find a job. He would depend on someone else's help all his life.

In Britain, we take eye tests for granted. If you need spectacles, you can get them on the National Health. Doctors and surgeons can perform near-miracles to save a person's sight. If you're unlucky enough to become blind, there are many ways you can be helped to live your life and have a job, not least through the Guide Dogs for the Blind Association.

In Malawi, there are only four eye doctors for the whole country. Fewer than ten per cent of the population regularly see an eye care specialist. And this is in a country where a poor diet and a shortage of clean water for washing make blindness ten times more likely to occur than in Britain.

Eye care specialist Dr Moses Chirambo, examining patients at Chiwaula – the first time these people had ever had their eyes seen by a doctor.

In some villages, the figures are even worse: between 20 and 40 times more people will be blind than in Britain.

Those are the kind of awful facts we gave when we launched the Sight Saver Appeal. We showed film of the kind of help that can begin to fight the battle against blindness in Africa. The main thing is for eye care experts to get out to the villages and to hold clinics to treat people with eye problems and to catch simple illnesses before they get any worse. In Africa, because of the lack of health care, a simple eye infection that would be cleared up in Britain by a dab of ointment can quickly lead to blindness. And

once someone's blind, there's often nothing to be done.

We wanted to provide two Mobile Eye Units to work in Malawi. They're Land Rovers – tough vehicles for tackling rugged ground – fully equipped with a portable eye clinic, all the instruments needed to perform on-the-spot examinations and even simple operations. The MEUs are manned by Ophthalmic Medical Assistants, who've been trained to deal with most types of eye disease and who can recognise more serious cases that need treatment back at the base hospital.

The experts who helped us plan and run the Sight Saver Appeal – the Royal Commonwealth Society for the Blind – worked out that the MEUs, all their equipment and the training of the Ophthalmic Assistants, would cost £100,000. But they also worked out that over the next seven years, which is as long as the vehicles last, they could

BLUE PETER SIGHT SAVERS APPEAL

HELP the fight for sight in Africa

Everyone at the BBC joined in! Phillip Schofield donated the jumper he'd been wearing when we launched the Appeal. Betty, our tea lady, sold Muesli fingers that Peter had made and raised £50!

13

Hundreds of people sent us pictures and photographs of their Sight Saver Bring & Buy Sales. The children in Mrs Burnell's Class sold orange juice and biscuits to the seniors.

All the children of North Farnborough Infant School took part. They raised £126.75.

help save the sight of 100,000 people. So when we launched the Appeal, we said: "Just £1 will save one person's sight!"

To raise the money, we decided to use the method we know works fastest – Bring and Buy Sales. The RCSB put together an excellent kit of posters, stickers and price lables for Bringers and Buyers and requests for the kit poured in as soon as we launched the Appeal. 5,000 went out in the first week, another 10,000 in the second. Altogether 37,000 Blue Peter Bring & Buy Sales were held all over the British Isles and in Germany, Holland, Belgium and Cyprus.

Meanwhile, we were lucky enough to get a first-hand account of the work of the eye care units. Mark went to Malawi with a Blue Peter film crew in November. He met Malawi's top eye doctor, Moses Chirambo, a brilliant, dedicated man who was to impress millions of viewers over the next few weeks. Moses showed Mark the kind of areas two new Mobile Eye Units would be operating in. They went to Chiwaula, a village that had never received a visit from an eye doctor before. People crowded round Moses and Mark, and even to Mark, it was obvious that many

had diseases like trachoma, where the eye seems to be red and swollen all the time, or were actually blind. Moses worked his way down a long, patient queue, handing out ointment and vitamin pills and giving advice about how to keep eyes clean and healthy. Then he spotted Emmanuel.

It was a lucky thing that Emmanuel's mother happened to bring him along. As he was already blind, she might have thought there was no point in spending a long afternoon waiting for him to be looked at. It was a miracle that the doctor who saw Emmanuel was Moses Chirambo. He examined Emmanuel carefully, looking long and hard into the boy's sightless eyes.

"There might just be something we can do for this chap," he said to Mark. It was possible, Moses explained, that a corneal graft operation might restore the sight in one of Emmanuel's eyes. It's a very delicate operation, especially when performed on young children. Moses thought there were no more than six surgeons in the whole world with a good chance of success in an operation like that. Fortunately, one of them, Dr Sam Levine, was working in Malawi for the RCSB at the time.

Moses explained the possibility of restoring Emmanuel's sight to his mother, and the need to take the little boy away from his home village for several weeks.

That first clinic in Chiwaula made a strong impression on Mark. The Appeal had been going very well even up to then, but once Mark's film was shown, thousands more requests for Bring and Buy Sale kits came in, and the amount raised shown on the Totalizer in

the studio went up in leaps and bounds. In less than a month, our original Target was reached and a new one, a much more ambitious one, was set: £500,000. That money would help eye care in three more countries – Nigeria, Tanzania and The Gambia – with more Mobile Eye Units and Medical Motorbikes. Caron went to paint the Blue Peter Ship on Malawi's first Land Rover and drove it into the container for the start of its long trip to Africa. It arrived there just after Christmas and went straight to work.

In January, we received the news that Emmanuel's operation was over, and the bandages were due to come off any day. So Janet went to Malawi to see our first Mobile Eye Unit in action, but most of all to meet the little boy who symbolized the help Blue Peter viewers were giving to Commonwealth Africa. She first saw him toddling up and down a corridor at Kamazu Central Hospital, chasing a ball.

That's a perfectly normal activity for most people, but pretty remarkable for someone who was blind the week before. The operation had been a complete success. Janet travelled with Emmanuel when Moses took him back to his village, over a day's drive away from the capital, Lilongwe. She saw him welcomed back into his family, knowing that because of the Sight Saver Appeal,

he is much more likely to live a happy and useful life.

The idea that just £1 could save someone's sight really hit home. The Bring and Buy Sales were a huge hit and it was with great joy that we drove four Mobile Eye Units (the fifth was the one already in Malawi – we had a lifesize cardboard cut-out to represent it!) and two Medical Motorbikes into the studio on January 5th 1987. You had done it! Not only that, the Totalizer had shot up to £1,000,000 – *ten times* the amount we'd originally asked for. Besides the vehicles, we could buy spares, build and equip an operating theatre in Tanzania, and pay for the all-important training of the Ophthalmic Medical Assistants to run the Mobile Eye Units. They are the key to the future. They have to teach the local people in the countryside how to look after themselves, to stop the spread of the crippling diseases which lead to blindness.

On behalf of Emmanuel, and all those other people whose sight will be saved over the next seven years – the young, the old, and those not even born yet – we say a heartfelt 'Thank you' to all Sight Savers.

P.S. By June 1987 the Sight Saver Appeal had raised nearly £2,000,000!

One million pounds and still counting! The studio is full of Mobile Eye Units and Medical Motorbikes – ridden by Caron and Dr Kenneth Kagame – on the day we reached our Sight Saver Target.

A Story with a Happy Ending. Two year old Emmanuel had his sight restored thanks to a corneal graft operation. He was able to see and clutch toys just days after the operation *(top)* Janet saw him welcomed back into his home a few days later *(bottom)* – the first person to have his sight saved thanks to Blue Peter viewers.

15

THE FOUR MILE FALL

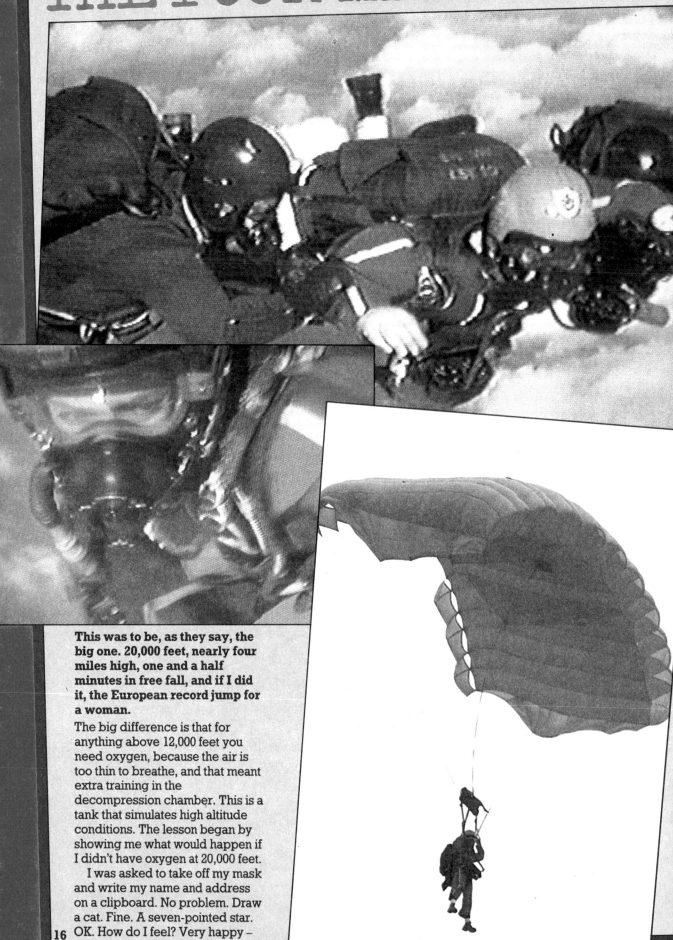

This was to be, as they say, the big one. 20,000 feet, nearly four miles high, one and a half minutes in free fall, and if I did it, the European record jump for a woman.

The big difference is that for anything above 12,000 feet you need oxygen, because the air is too thin to breathe, and that meant extra training in the decompression chamber. This is a tank that simulates high altitude conditions. The lesson began by showing me what would happen if I didn't have oxygen at 20,000 feet.

I was asked to take off my mask and write my name and address on a clipboard. No problem. Draw a cat. Fine. A seven-pointed star. OK. How do I feel? Very happy –

I learnt, not only how to use an oxygen mask, but about the extraordinary things that can happen to you *without* oxygen at 20,000 feet.

verging on the giggly in fact. Sitting with all those grown men drawing pussy cats made me fall about. Do it again? Anything you say. But it wasn't quite so easy the next time. My pussy cat turned out to be a very strange shape, and try as I might I just couldn't manage to write Janet Ellis.

I put the mask back on and after a few moments I was back to normal again, staring incredulously at the infantile scrawls I'd made

just a few seconds ago.

On October 8th, the weather was right, the wind speed was right, and the cloud base was right. I walked across the tarmac, climbed into the aircraft and took my position on the parachute seat that had almost become routine. I say, almost, because my stomach was telling me that four miles was a long, long way to fall!

Green light on. Go. We joined hands in our free fall positions – rocked forwards once and backwards once – and went for it.

I watched the vapour of the Hercules 20,000 feet above me, and remembered all the marvellous instructors who had made my free fall dream come true.

I rehearsed every move of our exit from the aircraft in a mock-up Hercules. Nothing is left to chance, because once you leave the real aircraft, there's no way back!

I can't describe what it's like being in free fall, except to say that it's the most wonderful experience in the world. It has the effect of causing time to stand still and the one and a half minutes feel as though they will go on forever.

I glanced at my altimeter. 4000 feet. I waved at the cameras. Bob and Terry swung away, and I pulled the ripcord.

The square canopy billowed out and I steered for the smoke flares, blowing across the distant dropping zone.

I hit the ground only a couple of metres from the target, which from 20,000 feet, wasn't bad. It had taken three and a half years of training, 33 actual jumps, a broken pelvis, and a good many moments I never want to experience again. But I wouldn't have missed it for the world!

P.S. Janet held the record from October 8th 1986 until March 11th 1987 when it was broken by Valerie Slattery and Francesca Gannon jumping from 25,300 feet.

the Famous Eight

HALLEY • BONZO • HONEY • FERGIE • SNOWY • AMBER • BONNIE • BRUNO

Goldie's second litter was born on February 3rd 1986. The pups' father is Zeke, a Guide Dogs for the Blind Association stud dog, and it's a great tribute to him and to Goldie that all the pups qualified as trainee Guide Dogs. Bonnie could have become one, too – but we kept her for our Blue Peter dog after her Mum retired when Simon became the programme's Countryside Correspondent.

These photos were both taken for the *Radio Times* and setting them up was far more tricky than filming a Duncan Dares! It was hard enough when the four dogs and four bitches were only five weeks old – but getting eight six month old Golden Retrievers to line up for the camera took a whole afternoon.

66,368 people sent in suggestions for names for the puppies, and we decided to call them after the most popular ideas.

Guide Dogs Puppy Walking Manager Derek Freeman lent us a hand when we named the pups. Our scrutineers sorted the 66,368 suggestions!

We liked Honey because that was the name of Blue Peter's very first Guide Dog, Fergie was in the news and so were Halley (the Comet) and Bruno (the Boxer). Amber was called after Goldie's Mum, Snowy suited the palest pup, Bonzo was the clown of the litter and Bonnie *was* just that!

It was Derek Freeman who picked out Bonnie as the pup best suited to be the new Blue Peter dog. He had come to put the whole litter through the very thorough tests the Guide Dogs for the Blind Association has to give any puppy before it's chosen for Puppy Walking training.

He examined each one to make sure there were no problems with eyes, ears, mouth or body. He had to check on how fearless each pup was – when Derek fires a gun, a puppy who cowers away can't be chosen. A nervous dog can never be a Guide Dog. Derek's such a wizard when it comes to dogs, his judgement is never wrong. It's thanks to his Breeding and Puppy Walking schemes that the Association successfully trains so many Guide Dogs.

Derek tested the pups and chose Bonnie to be our new Blue Peter dog. It wasn't long before she and Jack became good friends. This is the last photo taken before Jack died.

Bonnie's had some useful lessons from ex-Guide Dog Supervisor, Richard Duckworth. A great deal of animal training is common sense, but it's reassuring to have some expert advice.

For walking to heel, I began with the lead in my right hand and Bonnie on my left. I got her attention by slapping my thigh with my free left hand.

The secret with training any young puppy is a little and often. I learned to keep Bonnie's attention by my tone of voice. Whenever she did well, there was lots of praise!

HAPPY BIRTHDAY BONNIE

After a year of being 'puppy walked' – which means being looked after by a family chosen by the Association, and undergoing a fair amount of training, there are more tests and the trainees are sent away to school. We're all hoping the newest Blue Peter recruits will be successful. If they *are,* they'll bring the total of Blue Peter Guide Dogs to 34!

There's no doubt at all about Bonnie's success. This is largely due to some marvellous training tips from ex-Guide Dog Supervisor, Richard Duckworth.

Bonnie had been learning simple commands, 'sit' and 'stay' and 'come'. And Richard was pleased with her progress. Starting with the lead on – and a longish one is best for training – you hold it in your right hand (with the pup on your left) and you get the pup's attention by slapping your thigh with your free left hand.

"That's the secret," said Richard, "A slack lead and getting her attention the *whole* time. If the dog's bored, use your voice to get its attention back and give positive and lively commands."

Getting Bonnie to 'stay ', he walked away and left her for a few seconds. Then he walked towards her – turned – so they were both facing the same direction, then squatted down to her level with lots of "Well dones!" To let Bonnie know the exercise was finished, he stood up, with a final "Good girl!"

Bonnie wasn't the only one who learnt a lot from Richard – we all did. Now she's 17 months old and all those early lessons have paid off. Bonnie comes when she's called. She doesn't jump up, she doesn't scrounge for titbits and she walks to heel. It's good to see her following in Goldie's paw steps – Blue Peter dog number five is one the programme can be proud of!

Bonnie's brothers and sisters came to her first birthday party.

Compare Bonnie aged 4 weeks with this lovely photo taken when she was 7 months old.

20

Sliding into Blue Peter

There is more to working on Blue Peter than turning up twice a week in the studio – as Caron Keating, the latest recruit, was soon to discover.

"Just hang on tight, Caron," said Roger, "I don't want to win this race on my own!"

I thought they'd give me something nice and quiet for my first film.

"So you're the sort of girl who's willing to have a go at anything?"

"Well . . ? Yes!" I replied.

Who wouldn't? I was having an interview with Biddy Baxter, and if I did well I might get a job on Blue Peter. They probably wouldn't risk doing anything too elaborate with a new girl anyway.

Wrong!

I got the job. Great! But the ink was hardly dry on my contract before Biddy asked me if I'd like to have a go at Sidecar Racing.

"Sidecar racing?" I thought, "Doesn't sound all *that* difficult."

Wrong again!

The 'passenger' in a motor bike and sidecar race is the one who stops the whole vehicle from rolling over.

Roger Meason the British Masters champion told me exactly what my duties were going to be.

"All you have to do, Caron, is to ease out of the saddle as we approach the bend, and then lean out as far as you can so you can keep us on all three wheels."

What he didn't tell me was that we'd be doing 80 miles an hour across a sea of mud – and that my right knee was going to be centimetres from the ground.

But the key to it all was Roger Meason. He had that quiet confidence of someone who knows exactly what he's doing. And, even better, he was able to give *me* the confidence that with Roger in the saddle, everything was going to be OK.

"Any last minute tips?" I asked as he kicked the machine into life. He gave the machine a few aggressive revs.

"Just hang on tight, Caron. I don't want to win this race on my own."

I really wanted to do my best for Roger, but as well as being a complete novice I am also very light, so I would have to lean very far out if I was going to be any use at all.

The flag was down and we were off with engines roaring and mud flying in all directions. The first bend loomed up, and I moved my weight onto my right foot, grabbed the bar with my left hand – and leaned into the black wall of mud.

I did that 16 times and each one was more terrifying than the last. I felt that my strength was going, and I only hoped that my left arm would be good enough to keep me on the bike.

In the end we came second. More thanks to Roger's brilliant riding than to my 'passengering'. But I'd had a go, and I'd made my first Blue Peter film.

I hope that Biddy and the viewers thought it was alright.

CRAZY CRESS HEADS

Grow a Crazy Cress Head and you'll never be short of a sandwich filling! Every haircut gives you a snack – delicious with a hard-boiled egg or peanut butter.

HEAD

1 Loose woven cloth to allow the cress to grow through (if you use the knitted sort of dishcloth with two layers, trim off the edge all the way round and just use one layer).

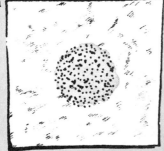

Lay the cloth flat. Sprinkle half a teaspoon of cress seed in the middle, in a circle.

2 Roll up four sheets of kitchen roll paper into a loose ball. Place it on the seeds very carefully without disturbing them.

3 Bring the corners up over the paper ball, bunching them together. Secure the bunch close to the paper ball with an elastic band (it doesn't matter if a few seeds drop through).

4 Fill a medium sized jar with water – a jam or pickle jar is ideal. Rest the head on the rim of the jar with the bunched material in the water.

5 Put the jar in a dark cupboard and leave it there until the seeds have begun to sprout (this will take 3 or 4 days). Take the jar out of the cupboard and stand it on a window sill. The leaves will be yellow at first, but after a couple of days they will turn green.

BODY

It can be tricky dressing the jar with water in it, so either dress another jar, or transfer the head into another jar and tip the water out of the original jar to dress it.

1 Cut away the foot and heel of an old sock and use the top of the sock to cover the jar.

2 Bring the cut edge of the sock over the top of the jar and tuck in any spare material. Bring the fold just below the rim (if it comes higher it will get wet from the head and absorb the water).

3 Half fill the jar with water and put the head in place.

FACE

1 Find the smoothest part of the head for the features. If there are any roots or leaves growing in the wrong place, just pull them out.

2 Cut shapes from felt or paper for the eyes and mouth. Simply press them onto the head (the damp material should hold them in position).

Once your Cress head has grown its cress 'hair' long enough you can give it a good hair cut and enjoy a snack!

ACCESSORIES

Use your imagination to turn your Cress Head into a character by adding a few buttons, a ruff, or perhaps a ribbon to the dress.

If you like, use kitchen foil for a space age Cress Head. Or, you could make a cheery red scarf from a tied handkerchief.

Dangly ear-rings can be made from small cut-up sections of a plastic drinking straw threaded together on a length of sewing thread and draped over the head.

You can make a pair of glasses by cutting the shape from a yoghurt pot. Colour them with a felt-tip pen and tie a piece of thin elastic at each side.

One day last year, there were monsters at the bottom of the Blue Peter garden! Not dinosaurs but great gleaming metallic beasts that roared and crunched and lumbered just as menacingly as any Tyrannosaurus Rex or Brontasaurus!

Just over our garden wall, there's the old White City site. The once famous Stadium – scene of the 1908 Olympic Games and thousands more sporting events and exhibitions – has been flattened by bulldozers and soon it'll be covered by new BBC TV studios and offices. But nothing seems to happen fast where builders and planners are concerned, so for a couple of years now, there's been this vast expanse of tarmac and churned up mud within a stone's throw of our garden.

And that proved to be a great stroke of luck when the organisers of the Truckfest '86 asked if we'd like to show Blue Peter viewers some of their Heavyweights of the Highway – a selection of the world's most advanced giant trucks and vans. There was no chance of driving them into our studio – they'd have sunk straight through the floor – so that's how the old stadium was turned into a race track for the very last time, for the stars of the trucking world. And with names like 'The Kenworth Wrecker', 'Land Train Tipper' and 'Super Monster', they sounded more like All-In Wrestling Champions than trucks!

Truckfest wasn't just

going to be a beauty parade – there were competitions, too, for the strongest, the most powerful and the most efficient of the vehicles. The Kenworth Wrecker turned out to be a gigantic rescue truck. It was a 12½ ton beast that could pull loads of 65 tons using a 16 speed gearbox. And its hydraulic lift raised damaged vehicles as effortlessly as though they were cotton wool balls.

The Land Train Tipper had hydraulics too – this time for transporting huge loads from

SUPER MONSTER

The owner of this Scania truck had it well and truly customised with paintings of harvest scenes!

sand and gravel pits. It was nicknamed 'Oasis' because of the beautiful picture painted on its side – and I soon discovered that this was how lots of the vehicles had been customised. Like the Scania truck that was decorated with harvest scenes – with horses pulling old fashioned threshing machines and modern combine harvesters.

"I think most Truck owners are very proud of their vehicles – they like to see them looking good," said Chris, the artist who'd painted the Scania.

"But why harvest scenes?" I asked.

"The owner sells tractors," explained Chris, "so he wanted pictures of the agricultural vehicles through the ages."

But all these stars faded into insignificance, compared with the vehicle Britain had waited ten years to see – Super Monster!

Built in America, it's the only one of its kind in Europe and its owner Jurg Dubler – who happens to be Swiss – explained why a rather ordinary looking truck had been perched on top of four gigantic tyres.

"In America, there might me a few million people who have trucks like this, for everyday use. Then they started to get them higher and higher up, so they could go through rougher country."

"What kind of wheels are they?" I wondered.

"On this one, the tyres are sand tyres that are used for digging oil in special places like Alaska or the desert. . ."

Whoops! I lurched sideways, as without warning, 'Super Monster' drove sideways like a crab.

"You feel like you're sliding," I gasped.

Jurg didn't bat an eyelid – driving sideways was nothing compared with Super Monster's next party piece.

I should have known something spectacular was up when I was told to put on a crash helmet, and Jurg drove towards two ordinary saloon cars, parked side by side.

"He can't have seen them," I thought, as Super Monster moved relentlessly forward. Then there was a crunch and a jerk and we were climbing! I couldn't believd it – there we were perched **on top** of the cars. And there we stayed – Super Monster had stalled!

Jurg wasn't pleased. He restarted the engine and we slithered down the other side of the cars – that were crushed like acorns by now. Then he began to reverse.

Apparently car crushing is all the rage in America – they even have car crushing races, and with so many vehicles bound for the scrapyards each year, it's as good a way of squashing them as any.

This time, I'll try and enjoy it, I thought, as Jurg revved up. This time we didn't stall – but I couldn't believe my ears.

"Not very good," muttered Jurg, after we'd pulverised the roofs and windscreens like squashing a couple of cockroaches.

"Why on earth not?"

"Because this car moved," replied Jurg, scowling as he pointed to the car on the left. What a perfectionist! The movement couldn't have been more than a few centimetres. But Jurg wasn't satisfied and we moved menacingly forward towards a second pair of cars. This time we hammmered in chocks to stop them moving. And just to make doubly sure, I checked the handbrakes were on and stuck both cars in reverse gear.

"OK – I try!" said Jurg, and we were up and over once more. Third time lucky – Jurg actually smiled. I looked at the lumps of mangled metal that were once cars and made a vow. If I meet Jurg the next time he's in Britain, I'll make sure *my* car isn't parked within 100 miles!

LAND OF HOPE AND GLORY

If you work on Blue Peter, sooner or later you can fulfill every ambition you ever had. Free fall parachuting, cleaning the clockface of Big Ben, diving on the *Mary Rose* – you name it, we've done it. It was in the middle of free fall training that another completely different and equally terrifying idea struck me. *I wanted to sing with the BBC Symphony Chorus on the Last Night of the Proms.*

One of my secret ambitions has been to sing with the BBC Symphony Chorus on the Last Night of the Proms at the Royal Albert Hall.

This is one of those very English occasions, which takes place every September at the Royal Albert Hall in London. It marks the end of a series of concerts that have been held every year since 1895. They are called 'promenade' concerts because you can buy a cheap ticket and stand up to hear the music and in between the pieces you can stroll about or 'promenade' and chat to your friends.

The last night is a party night, with rousing choral numbers like *Land of Hope and Glory* and *Jerusalem*. A lady comes on and sings *Rule Britannia* and the promenaders go wild. This is the British sending themselves up for being so patriotic but really loving every minute of it.

The BBC Symphony Chorus hold auditions from time to time, so I went along to try my luck. Gareth Morell, the Chorus Master, and Bob Ben, the Chorus Secretary, were very nice to me because I came from Blue Peter, but they

were obviously not going to clutter up their choir with a load of rubbish. I had prepared a song from Mozart's opera 'The Marriage of Figaro'. It has a lovely melody and it sounds very easy when someone else sings it but, I realised, far too late, that it was a very tricky piece of music indeed... Gareth was extremely polite, but I knew it wasn't very good.

The next bit was even worse!

"Janet – we'd just like to check up on your sight reading," said Gareth, putting a piece of music I'd never seen before on my music stand. The piano began and with a trembling forefinger, I followed the notes across the page. When we reached the words I realised they were in Latin! I struggled

My first audition was a disaster! They told me to come back when I'd had some training.

Biddy sent me to Vera Rozsa, who is one of the most famous singing teachers in Britain.

through the first couple of lines, but soon I was left gulping whilst the piano thundered on as a solo to the end.

"You've got quite a nice voice," Gareth said, "but it's obviously a bit rusty, and you'll need to do some work on your sight reading before we can offer you a place in the Chorus."

I went back to the Blue Peter office and reported my failure to Biddy, who said,

"If your voice needs training, we'll send you to the best singing teacher in Britain!"

So the next day I was at the studio of Vera Rozsa, who teaches Kiri Te Kanawa and many other famous opera singers. We had another go at the Mozart, with Vera lifting my head, tapping my diaphragm, and saying, "Relax, enjoy the music!"

Slowly I began to feel a bit more confident. Vera was very tough, but very encouraging, and I could feel myself getting better.

We swapped the Mozart for Gilbert and Sullivan which, if not better, was certainly easier, and my confidence grew, until I felt strong enough to face Gareth again.

I think he was quite surprised at the improvement. Instead of trembling quietly, my voice seemed really to fill the room.

Gareth told me he was looking forward to seeing me at rehearsals! *I was in!*

**The conductor raised his baton and we sang with all our might:
"Land of Hope and Glory Mother of the Free,..."**

REHEARSAL IN PROGRESS

The next few weeks were a frantic round of dashing from the Television Centre after Blue Peter to take my place amongst the 190 members of the BBC Symphony Chorus. Every note, every pause, every intonation and every consonant, was rehearsed over and over again, until Gareth felt we were good enough to meet Vernon Handley, the conductor.

He turned out to be absolutely charming, as he moulded what was, by now, a very competent performance into the sound that he wanted to hear on the night.

That feeling of terror mixed with excitement that every performer knows started about a mile before I reached the Albert Hall, as I joined all the crowds of bizarrely-dressed young people converging on the door. I made for

My next audition was successful – and soon I was rehearsing with the famous choir.

the entrance marked 'Artistes only', gripping my carrier bag containing my freshly ironed evening dress.

Once through the door, I met a cacophony of sound that set my pulses racing – 100 instruments, warming up, and practising their individual tricky bits – voices of every range running up and down scales, men frantically tying their bow ties, and girls squeezing into their smooth black dresses.

I joined the queue behind my fellow sopranos, and soon I was walking into that vast arena, and hearing the applause roaring round the hall like an incoming tide.

I sat through the other pieces in the concert without hearing them. Then Vernon, now resplendent in a white dinner jacket, waved us to our feet. I took a deep breath, and with 190 of my new colleagues, belted out:

"Land of Hope and Glory, Mother of the Free, How shall we extoll them, Who are born of thee?"

I remember thinking that the only thing that could top this experience, would be doing it free fall! And what a good thing that it was impossible, because the excitement would probably have made me burst!

THE REAL THING

The double life of Chris Amoo

February 9th 1987
Chris shows some of the prizes won by Gable and Solace.

There can't be many pop stars who breed Afghan hounds as a hobby – there's only one in the world whose dog beat 14,500 competitors to become Crufts Supreme Champion!

For Chris Amoo of The Real Thing a dream came true on February 15th 1987. Only a week before the contest all dog breeders would give their left arm to win, The Real Thing performed 'live' on Blue Peter. Lead singer Chris, introduced us to Champion Viscount Grant – or Gable for short and Gable's sister Sade Solace. "I just love their temperament and their whole character," said Chris, who had his first Afghan as a pet, eight years ago, and now owns five of them.

Although Gable was only two and Solace just nine months, they'd both won stacks of trophies and rosettes. Gable had been the Yorkshire Afghan Hound Society's Pup of the Year in 1985 and Top Afghan in 1987 – now there was "the big one" – the world's biggest dog show!

"I think Gable stands as good a chance as any," Chris said modestly. Little did he know!

As he ran round the studio with Gable positively gliding by his side, Chris explained the judges looked for Afghans with a nice springing movement. "They should look as if they're running on a cushion of air – and they want to be very proud – very arrogant as though they own the ring!"

A week later and Gable *did* own the ring and the crowds cheered as Chris and Gable were presented with the Supreme Champion's colossal silver cup! The next day Chris returned to the Blue Peter studio in a daze. "I'm still on Cloud 9," he grinned. When did he get the first inkling Gable was in with a chance?

"When he won the Hound Group," Chris replied. "I thought – there are only five to beat now –

6 days later – Gable became Britain's Top Dog!

that's better than 14,500!"

But all the same, Chris never *really* believed Gable would win – it's only the second time an Afghan has been Supreme Champion in the whole history of Crufts. What of the future? "He's part of the family," said Chris. "He's a pet dog first and a Show dog second."

That's what we all liked about Gable – it's not very often that a real family pet becomes Top Dog at Crufts.

Living Paintings

A bunch of flowers added a splash of colour to Chris Knott's frame.

How many times have *you* been to an exhibition when a painting hit you? . . . or ate a banana? . . . or took your glasses off?

Sprayed in purple paint, Stephen Taylor-Woodrow and Daniel Kay (bright pink!) stay "framed" for as long as eight hours.

You never know what's going to happen next on Blue Peter – and sometimes it's just as well!

"We're having a few paintings in on Monday," was the casual remark made by Biddy Baxter after one of the Thursday programmes.

"Oh great," Pete said. "A nice bit of culture, I fancy Van Gogh myself."

"Who painted all those beautiful horses . . . George Stubbs? I love those," said Janet.

"Give me Picasso any day," said Mark. "All those faces with five noses and the bright colours – brilliant!" We wondered why she smiled.

'Living Paintings' weren't anything like any other works of art – classical or modern – we'd ever seen.

With these pictures, it's the artists who are hung up! And what's more – they stay hung up

for anything up to eight hours at a time. And it's not a joke. Stephen Taylor-Woodrow, who sprays himself from head to toe with purple paint says, "In order to fully understand the nature of a

30

All hung up and striking a pose! Peter volunteered to become a 'Living Painting' – with a little help from his friends.

can't go to the lavatory whilst they're being paintings. But they do eat – and it's a spooky effect when a painted face demolishes a chicken leg or a jam butty. At one stage the grey painting peeled a banana and stuffed it in his mouth. But we didn't think much of their table manners – the banana skin, chicken bone and cardboard plate came whizzing past our ears as they were chucked across the studio, (the banana skin landed on a camera!)

But you can't really understand a 'Living Painting' until you become one. So in the cause of art, that's what Peter volunteered to do – kitted out in special shoes that took most of his weight when he was hung up, and a harness under his jacket that we fixed to hooks concealed behind his back.

He decided on a Maradona pose – so we added a football to the frame and the finished effect looked pretty good. Pete liked it a lot – until he realised we were going to keep him hung up all through an eight minute film!

"I don't know how they stick it for eight hours," he gasped when we took pity on him and un-hooked him.

'Living Paintings' don't only exhibit themselves in art galleries. They say that anyone can hire them to hang in their living rooms at home. But it's quite a carry on, because apart from decorating their picture frames – which takes three hours, it takes another two hours to spray their paint on.

But meeting them is an experience not to be missed. And if like us, you're dying to know how on earth they do hold out for eight hours – the answer is they don't. There are bottles in strategic positions under their trousers!

and fast.

Stephen, Chris and Daniel have a strict rule they never, ever utter a word while they're hung up. And it's really weird to talk to people who've been having normal conversations when their feet were on the ground, who stare blankly ahead of them as though they were completely invisible.

But they do more. "Ouch!" yelled Pete as unsuspectingly, standing just in front of the grey 'Living Painting', he received a thump on the head. Quick as a flash, there was a long pink arm round Mark's neck and fat thick pink fingers removed his specs and put them on the painting's nose!

That's another speciality – the paintings have real live accessories – a vase of flowers say, or a few apples, stuck on their frames, like giant collages.

Then Mark was lifted up while the purple painting bent down and gave a very surprised Bonnie, a pat!

It takes tremendous concentration to stay in fixed positions for hours on end.

For one thing, Stephen, Daniel and Chris

painting, it is necessary to become a painting."

And when he and fellow 'Living Paintings' Daniel Kay (in bright pink) and Chris Knott (a tasteful shade of pale grey) exhibited themselves at the Wolverhampton Art Gallery, the place was packed with over 15,000 visitors in five days which was more than the Gallery usually gets in six months.

From the moment the paintings were hung on their heavy wooden frames along the back of our studio, the surprises came thick

THE RELUCTANT DAREDEVIL

The Side-on Drive: all in a day's work for Joe . . .

I didn't even know where I was going as I was helped, or bundled, into a car by a burly BBC Commissionaire. When we reached the outskirts of Wimbledon, I cheered up a lot. Wimbledon means tennis, and I *love* tennis. But we didn't go to the All-England Lawn Tennis Club, we stopped at Wimbledon Common. Then we drove right into a topsy-turvy world where lots of ordinary things were behaving in a most unusual manner. There was a car driving past, balanced on two wheels. There was a motorbike, being driven *backwards.* I got out of the car, and had a crash helmet tossed into my hands.

"Help," I said. And I meant it.

I had been invited to spend the day with the famous Hollywood Display Team, who tour the world with a dazzling show of stunts on cars and motorbikes. The performers are all experienced stunt drivers, and their skills have added the sparkle to countless car chases in films and TV series. This was one invitation I felt like refusing, but I soon realised that these characters were top-class experts and wouldn't expect me to

do anything that wasn't tried and tested. All I had to conquer were my own nerves.

So it was on with the helmet, and into the white Toyota for the Side-on Drive. The car drives up a ramp which raises the passenger side up into the air, and the skill of the driver keeps it there. It's incredibly difficult but Joe managed the trick perfectly. And I soon got used to looking at the world from an angle of 45 degrees.

Next stop – the motorbike. This felt very weird – perched on the back, looking backwards while the bike went forwards. Sitting behind me (which was really in

front of me) was Steve Flaherty, who had a perfect sense of balance, and made it seem like normal bike riding. I started to relax and I even managed to raise one arm off the seat in a sort of wave to the camera. But the next trick brought all my nerves back again.

It was a kind of tightrope act. All I had to do was sit tight on a frame. The trouble was that the frame was suspended from a bike which Steve was going to ride along a cable, 30 metres up in the air. If that wasn't enough, two of the girls from the team would be hanging onto the side of the frame. The

only things that would stop the whole contraption from crashing to the ground were the motorbike wheels and the skill of the rider. There was one more small point. I'm absolutely terrified of heights.

All dressed up and somewhere to go: Curry looks confident, but is terrified.

I've got vertigo, which means I get dizzy going up a ladder. It took a lot of persuading before I agreed to do it. I thought I could always shut my eyes, and nobody would ever know.

So up we went, up to where I felt certain we'd soon bump into a cloud. Steve drove straight and true, the cable was as steady as a rock, and I sat there waiting for it to end. Did I shut my eyes? I'm not telling. Truth is, I can't remember. Anyway, after what seemed like about a day-and-a-half, we came down. I felt great. Me, a lifetime vertigo sufferer, had been clinging onto a tiny metal frame, 30 metres up in the air. Would I do it again? Not on your life.

I was so relieved to have got that over that I was ready to agree to anything they wanted, so long as it was on the ground. I was still in a daze, as Dave Thurston, the leader of the Display Team, stuck an extra-thick balaclava helmet

over my head. He lifted me up and plonked me, tummy first, onto the bonnet of a car.

"What's this, Dave? What's it all about?"

"You'll see".

I soon saw well enough. Ahead of the car was a little wooden wall, about two metres wide. I saw Dave walk up to it with a burning torch. With a soft *woomph,* it went up in flames. I was about to be used as a human battering ram. It all happened so quickly, I had no time to worry about it. The car accelerated. I put my head down, we smashed through the wall, scattering the flaming wood in all directions, and the stunt was over. There wasn't a mark on me.

I take my balaclava helmet off to the Hollywood Display Team. If someone had told me what I'd be getting up to in the course of a single day, I never would have believed them. They are experts who certainly know their jobs. But was I glad to see the back of them! And the next time I go to Wimbledon, I'm taking my tennis racquet, and I'm not going anywhere near the Common!

I hope you like your Curry hot, because that's how they serve them in Hollywood.

33

SIMON'S HARVEST FESTIVAL

Last year Simon Groom left **Blue Peter** to return to his first love, the countryside, and to spend more time on the farm where he was born in Derbyshire. But he's kept in touch and in the gaps between lambing and ploughing and harvesting, he spares time to send us his countryside reports.

I remember my Mother and my Auntie Barbara getting onto a bagger-combiner at eleven o'clock one Friday morning and getting off at half past one the following day. There's no knocking off time at the harvest, not until you fall off the harvester in sheer exhaustion. It's the climax of the farming year. Everything you've worked for since ploughing and drilling in the winter and the spring is suddenly there, and must be gathered. Tomorrow the weather might change and the whole lot could be ruined.

There's a tingle of excitement when you wake up seeing the sun glinting on the golden corn and you know that this is the day. It is something that every farmer knows and looks forward to every year. I believe the thrill is the same whether you're ringing up to book the combine harvester, or going off to sharpen the scythes and sickles and bagging hooks as they did 200 years ago.

In those days the farmer would have employed armies of workers to reap and bind and gather in the harvest by hand. When it was all over they would have a great feast for the whole community and then, on Sunday they would all go to church to thank God for the harvest and sing:

"All is safely gathered in
'Ere the winter storms begin".

The invention of the reaper was the first great breakthrough. With a team of shire horses one man could cut a field of corn on his own. He still needed a gang of people to gather and bind and stack, but this was the beginning of mechanised farming and a head start in the race against the old enemy, the weather.

The binder was an even better invention. This was a machine that bound the corn into sheaves and tossed them clear of the horses'

At the National Shire Horse Centre Nigel Flower introduced me to his team of giants: Sovereign, Emperor and Baron.

How's this for a hoof? It belongs to Sovereign and it measures an unbelievable 21 inches (over 50 centimetres) across!

path ready for the workers to stack them into stooks which dried in the wind. This is how things are still done at the National Shire Horse Centre which is where I went to see for myself what harvesting was like in the old days. Nigel Flower introduced me to his team.

"This is Sovereign. He's the one who wants to do all the work – that's why he's got such a sweat on – and Baron, who's a much calmer horse, and Emperor who is the real leader."

My grandfather was a blacksmith so I've always had an interest in shire horses. There's a sort of gentleness about them in spite of their overbearing size and strength. Their hoofs are unbelievable – Sovereign's shoe measured 8 inches, (over 21 centimetres) across!

Nigel let me reap a line or two of corn which I found much more of a test than driving the combine we hire on the farm at home. There is a great deal of machinery between the driver and the horse's rump. This makes keeping the team on line, so that you aren't missing any

The binder was tricky to drive, but it was a great leap forward in its day – cutting the corn, binding it into sheaves, and tossing them out of the horse's way.

corn, much more difficult than it looks.

The roar of the steam engine shattered the tranquillity of the countryside and took farming into the industrial age. There could be no way back.

But the days of the shire horse were numbered, and the first roar of the steam engine took farming into the industrial age. Great steam tractors were driven into the field to power the threshers that gobbled up the sheaves of corn, spat out the straw at one end and poured the precious grain into sacks at the other.

With the clamour of the engines disturbing the tranquillity of the countryside, people must have thought that farming would never be the same again. But there was one more monster to come that would revolutionise harvesting. The single machine that would do everything.

I went to a field in Essex to drive the biggest combine harvester in the world. There I sat, four metres off the ground, in air-conditioned splendour, listening to the radio, whilst below me this magnificent machine cut and threshed and stored 9350 litres of grain in its tank, as it blew out the chaff and straw in a dust cloud behind me. When the tank was full I radioed for a tractor. It drove alongside me as I extended the grain chute and emptied out eight tonnes of grain without a second's pause in the reaping.

It took just two men a couple of days where 100 years ago it would have been 50 men working for a couple of weeks. The terror of the weather is all but beaten. But there is a cost. Unemployment is just as harsh in the country as it is in the town and the new machinery has cut manpower to the minimum.

The massive combines need space, so hedgerows have been uprooted to make room for the machinery and to make more efficient use of the land. The hedgerows were once homes for thousands of birds, insects, and animals. The ones that survive are often poisoned by the pesticides and fertilisers needed to produce such bumper crops. But on top of all that, many people think that this country produces too much grain anyway, and tonnes of it end up being stored in huge grain mountains.

The combine has made farming a thousand times more efficient than it was at the beginning of the century, but it has made it a lonely

Steam could power machines that could gobble up the sheaves of corn, and separate the straw from the grain at the same time.

Today the huge combine harvesters can do everything, bar actually baking the bread!

The driver in his luxurious air-conditioned cab, does the work of 50 people. Without even raising a sweat!

life. At dinner time on the great prairie farm in Essex I ate my sandwiches alone in my super comfortable air-conditioned cab, but at the National Shire Horse Centre I sat in a corner of the field with half a dozen other workers as we washed down our dinners with

a mug of cider and swapped harvest stories for half an hour.

And when I went back to work Emperor and Sovereign and Baron gave me a much warmer welcome than the £100,000 monster machine in Essex.

A welcome break at the Shire Horse Centre. Driving the combine was an easier but a lonelier job. Maybe we've become too efficient, providing more grain than we need, and destroying the countryside in the process.

The Grand Tour

I'd like to bet that somewhere at home, you've got a souvenir of a day trip or a holiday. A stick of Blackpool or Great Yarmouth rock, decorated shells or pebbles or maybe a miniature Eiffel Tower or a Spanish doll, if you're lucky enough to have been abroad. And there's nothing new about holiday souvenirs – they've been around for hundreds of years – and sometimes they've turned out to be a colossal problem.

200 years ago it was the custom for the son of a wealthy family to be sent to travel abroad with a tutor. The trip was partly educational, like a school journey, and it was called the 'Grand Tour'.

For clever boys, it was very exciting. They all learned Latin and Greek at school in those days, so if they travelled as far as Italy or Greece, they were very interested to see the ancient buildings and the sites of the battles they had read about.

37

It made the adventures of the classic heroes really come alive, to read them again in the very places where they had once lived, and they were thrilled to see statues, columns and ruins that were thousands of years old.

And if these antique treasures were offered for sale, the rich young men bought them eagerly. In those days there were no laws to stop this, and it was splendid to take a real Roman statue back home!

The Grand Tour lasted at least a year, and that was a lot of time for collecting. And at the end, there was an enormous stack of antique souvenirs to be shipped home – enough to remind the young man of his travels for the rest of his life!

When he got home, the packing cases and parcels arrived too, and he unpacked them in great excitement. His parents were delighted to see their son again, but they were not so pleased to see how much he had brought home from his 'Grand Tour'. They wondered what on earth they would do with all the souvenirs!

Luckily most of the young men who went on the Grand Tour came from rich families who lived in stately homes. And often the easiest thing was to give up a whole room to turn into a museum, full of the young master's collection of classical antiquities.

Of course, like holiday souvenirs today, some were so lovely the family was really pleased. It was wonderful to see a helmet made 600 years before the birth of Christ, and fascinating to wonder who the warrior was who wore it, and what battles he fought!

And anyone would be delighted with a tiny bronze panther cub, made in Rome nearly 2,000 years ago. Both these treasures still belong to the families of the two young men who made the Grand Tour, 200 years ago.

But sometimes they really did go too far!

One of them brought back a foot! A colossal right foot carved from Egyptian volcanic stone, nearly 2,000 years previously. He probably found it in Italy, but no one knows why on earth it was made in the first place, or why anyone should want to bring it all the way back to England. It weighs a massive one tonne, and wondering where to put it when it arrived, must have been a problem for the stateliest home!

200 years ago it belonged to the Earl of Besborough and since then it's changed hands several times – once, it's said, for as little as £25 – the owner was probably glad to get rid of it!

But now it's on permanent loan to the Greek Museum at Newcastle University. So you might say that after all its travels, the foot is in safe hands at last!

Two historic Grand tour treasures – a bronze helmet made in 600 BC and a 2,000 year old bronze panther.

One of the biggest and heaviest of all holiday souvenirs! It took four men and a forklift truck to carry this gi-normous right foot into our studio.

UP TELECOM TOWER...

It helps to have a head for heights on Blue Peter. You never know when it might come in useful. Like the day I went to change the aerials three-quarters of the way up the famous Telecom Tower in London.

The aerial level of the Telecom Tower. The older, angular aerials are gradually being replaced by the new round ones.

The aerials are those large round things on the side of the tower, not a bit like an ordinary television aerial. These aerials are used to send and relay thousands of telephone calls and several channels of television pictures all over the country at the same time. The old aerials were those very distinctive rectangular ones that were put up when the Tower was built 21 years ago. They can't cope any more with the much larger number of phone calls we all need to make nowadays, so over the last few years, British Telecom has been replacing them with the latest technology. But even the latest technology needs a good old fashioned kick in the pants to get it going, and there's no mystery about how a hi-tech lump of ironmongery gets 200 metres up into the air . . . you haul it up on the end of a gi-normous crane.

But before you can hoist your aerial, you've got to build your crane. 170-metre-tall cranes aren't an everyday sight on the streets of London, and getting up one is quite an operation in itself. The night before, the police closed all the surrounding roads and 24 lorries began arriving, each lorry carrying one section of the crane. The sections were laid end-to-end and bolted together. Then a series of smaller cranes hoisted the whole thing up above the London skyline. The crane had to be very precisely positioned on the road. A few centimetres out, and when it swung round it would be in danger of clobbering a passing skyscraper. So I paid special

Two giants meet. That little speck hanging from the jib of the tower crane is a one tonne, four metre diameter aerial.

attention as the network of cables, pulleys and counterweights brought the great beast to life. I knew that pretty soon, I'd be dangling from that crane and I had every reason to make sure it was going to work properly.

The first job, once the crane was safely up, was nipping up to the top of the Tower to pick up a rope. One end would remain up there, with the gang of riggers, who would use it to haul in the aerial. This would be hanging on the other end, suspended from the crane. Got it? Simple, really. One snag, though – the rope had to come down the Tower on the *outside*. You couldn't just nip up in the lift with it.

So Brian Piercy, the Heavy Lift Manager (what a great job description!), Steve Bennett, our cameraman, and I all got into the little metal basket and clipped our safety harnesses on to the main crane cable above our heads.

As we got ready to be hauled up, the twin attractions of something usual happening in a crane basket, and the Blue Peter filming had caused quite a crowd to gather. I felt like an early intrepid balloonist as we swung off the ground, accompanied

40

change from being reassuringly strong into a spider's web. Funny how your view of something can alter your ideas. But these were temporary nerves which soon passed, and I concentrated on the job in hand.

Where a Blue Peter presenter goes, the cameraman has to go as well. At least I could hold onto the side of the basket with both hands. Steve had to have both hands on his film camera. But he did a great job, and during our ride he captured some of the most stunning pictures of London and the Telecom Tower that anyone has ever seen.

We were being lifted at a safe distance from the Tower to stop us banging into it, but as we reached the right height, Brian gave precise instructions to the crane driver over the walkie-talkie. We edged closer into the aerial level of the Tower, and I could make out the faces of the men who were getting ready to throw us the rope. It was very quiet, except for the crackle of Brian's radio, and it felt like we were docking with an orbiting space station. And as we swung in, I caught sight of our

We carefully clipped on our safety harness before the crane basket left the ground.

What a view! The London skyline makes a spectacular backdrop as we are lifted over 100 metres into the air.

by a ragged cheer from the spectators. But in a few seconds, the sounds from the pavement died away as we went higher and higher, getting our first look at the spectacular panoramic views across London.

As we went up, we also got a good look at the crane which was lifting us. The sections might look like fairly solid chunks of steel when you're down on the ground, but when you're suspended from a crane, they take on the appearance of fragile lengths of gossamer, likely to crumple in anything stronger than a summer breeze. And suddenly the cable we were hanging from seemed to

Not many reporters have ever been in this position! While I talk to the camera on the Tower, the cameraman, Steve Bennett looks through his viewfinder and the Heavy Lift Manager, Brian Piercy gives walkie-talkie instructions to the crane driver. We felt very small in that basket with the city swinging about far below us.

second camera, high on the Tower itself, and talking to it, I did one of the most unusual pieces-to-camera of my entire career.

And with a thump the rope thudded against the basket and I grabbed it with both hands. Mission accomplished! Brian handed the walkie-talkie to me, so I could direct the crane driver to let us down.

"Right, Stan," I said, "We've got the rope. You can put us down now, into the rope."

There was a pause.

"Not the rope, you wally. Into the road," said Brian.

"Oh, sorry. Into the road," I said into the radio.

And with the rope firmly in my grasp, we began the long trip back to the ground. With pinpoint accuracy, we were put down in exactly the place that we'd left. The first aerial was secured to the crane's hook, the rope tied on, and off it went. This time, the basket had to stay on the ground, but I wanted to be up at the top to meet the aerial coming in, so this time I took a short cut and went up the Tower the sensible, but slightly boring, way compared to the basket – in the express lift.

When I emerged onto the tiny

Left hand down a bit! The aerial inches its way to its home on the side of the Tower.

gantry where the rigging team were getting ready, the aerial itself was still some way off, but gradually it approached, dangling tantalizingly close to its new home. You felt like you could reach out and touch it. You couldn't, of course, not without leaping a 20 metre gap. Anyway, I had my safety harness to stop me trying.

With incredible timing and control, the crane driver, who was sitting 150 metres away, brought the aerial dish in, following more instructions given over the radio. The gang hauled away on the top to tease and coax the aerial into its precise place on the side of the Tower. I found I was perched right over one of the bolt holes it had to be secured to, so with bolt in hand I waited for exactly the right moment, then rammed it home. The aerial was up.

Mission accomplished! A snap of one newly-installed and positioned aerial dish and one very proud and happy newly-experienced rigger.

It had been a terrific operation, lasting 18 hours from when the police closed the road, to me slotting in that bolt. Despite the complexities of first building the crane, and then hoisting the one-tonne four-metre dish, there hadn't been the slightest hitch. And now that aerial is part of the network that links millions of telephones and televisions. Occasionally, when I'm on the phone, I think about my aerial and wonder if it's listening to my voice. And there's nothing better than driving past the Telecom Tower, glancing up, and thinking: "I've been up-there . . . on the *outside!*"

It is the Spring of 1888 and a fine Victorian lady and a noble gentleman meet at one of the popular English inland resorts. It is at Malvern that Miss Ellis is introduced to Mr Groom and together they decide to pass a pleasant week...

TAKING THE WATERS...

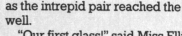

Malvern is one of the country's major Spa towns. There are natural freshwater springs in the hills, and the wealthy, fat Victorians came here in droves – taking advantage of Mr Brunel's Great Western Railway. Spa treatments were very highly thought of in Victorian times. They believed water most beneficial to the body.

And that was how Miss Ellis and Mr Groom came to be standing alongside each other one morning, dressed in the latest Victorian bathing costumes, with Miss Ellis daringly revealing a glimpse of handsome calf, just above her ankle.

Without warning, SPLOOSH, a stream of icy Malvern water landed on each of their heads.

"Good grief, Miss Ellis, what was that?" said the drenched Mr Groom.

"That, Mr Groom," said the equally bedraggled Miss Ellis, "was the Descending Douche."

"Ah. Most refreshing."

The next stage in the treatment was the application of cold wet towels to one's person. Eager Spa assistants – some a bit too eager – pressed forward with the sodden towels and wrapped the unfortunate pair tightly in them.

"How long must one stay like this, Doctor?"

"One hour," said the Doctor, sternly.

"Are you sure this is efficacious, Doctor?" said Miss Ellis.

"Definitely. Especially for rheumatism and gout."

"What – it gives you rheumatism and gout?" said the doubting Groom.

"No, it cures it."

If you don't think you could stick this cold torture for a whole hour, there were plenty of strict Victorians watching to make sure you did! This, believe it or not, was the height of expensive luxury.

And after the cold sheets and a colder shallow bath, there was the donkey ride into the beautiful Malvern Hills. The destination was St Ann's Well, a spring of purest water, discovered 700 years ago. Up here, you cleaned out the remaining impurities in your body with *ten* glasses of water. This was so highly thought of, that even Queen Victoria tried it when she was a girl.

"At last!" exclaimed Mr Groom,

as the intrepid pair reached the well.

"Our first glass!" said Miss Ellis, as the pair toasted each other's health. "It's most refreshing."

"How many glasses?" she enquired a little later on.

"Ten. That was number five."

"Goodness me," said the polite young lady. "I feel replete already."

But they stuck it out, even as the first flush of enthusiasm was replaced by the first flush of the bladder. If they felt a little full, they carried on, because they could *feel* the good it was doing them. It took more than a few glasses of water to crush the resolve of our ancestors.

And once the Victorians had taken the waters, what better than a little light exercise? They strode out across the Malvern Hills – just a brisk ten miles or so – to get the blood circulating. This was the answer to all that stodgy greasy food they used to eat. And it was worth paying a small fortune to breathe the fresh Worcestershire air and to drink at Nature's Spring.

At the end of the day, having been bathed, douched, drunk ten glasses of water, walked around the county and had a final immersion, the Victorians might try the Spa Treatment from Bath: 20 buckets of water for a penny. By now Miss Ellis and Mr Groom – dressed once more in their still-soaking costumes – knew what to expect. But they took it like the Empire builders they were.

SPLOOSH! SPLOOSH!! SPLOOSH!!!

Place: Droitwich, Worcestershire
Date: Late 1980s

Janet Ellis and her friend Simon Groom decide to fight their flab in the latest, most scientific way yet invented, and perfected here at the saltwater spa of Droitwich – by hydrotherapy – the application of water to the body. Yes, spas are back in fashion again, and water is all the rage. You might think it's a far cry from Malvern's heyday. You'd be wrong. There's still exercise – and plenty of it – but these days they have *scientific* ways of measuring your fat.

Fitness management experts define your bodily state and work out a programme for your treatment. One of the experts approached Janet with a pair of callipers. He grasped her arm, the fleshy part just above the elbow.

"This, we tend to find, is the best way of measuring fat in ladies," he

explained.

"Charming," said Janet.

The expert fiddled about with his measurements for a minute.

"From that we get a reading of five. About average."

"Do you want to measure my arm," Simon volunteered.

"We find that in gentlemen, it's the fat along the lower back which gives the most accurate reading."

"Come on, Groom, reveal the manly torso," encouraged Janet.

"Watch where you're going with those callipers." More fiddling about. Then the expert said,

"That's a reading of 14. About right for someone your age."

Simon didn't know whether to look happy or sad as he absorbed this piece of information.

But Droitwich's pride and joy is its saltwater swimming pool. There's so much salt found naturally in the water that even non-swimmers can float easily. It's marvellous for the treatment of ill or handicapped people who have trouble moving around. You just walk in – or get lowered in – lift up your legs and you're floating. It's a feeling of weightlessness, like being up in space. Once Janet and Simon got used to it, they spent hours in there, doing all manner of exercises prescribed by the fitness management experts.

Droitwich is ultra-modern, with every conceivable device on hand to make your body lean and healthy. And when you think about it, that's exactly what they were doing at Malvern 100 years ago. We might think the Victorian love affair with cold baths a bit strange. But were they any stranger than cavorting about in the incredibly salty water that bubbles up from the ground at Droitwich?

And in 100 years' time, will *our* great-great-grandchildren watch old film of today's spas and have a giggle at the way their ancestors did things – back in the quaint old 1980s?

Birds' Banquet

Don't let the wild birds suffer in freezing weather. Regular feeding can save thousands of lives and you don't need to buy expensive bird food. The Blue Peter Winter Bird Cake has been a sure fire success over the years and our friends from the Bentworth Primary School Bird Patrol have adapted it for small quantities – useful if you don't have a lot of leftovers and kitchen scraps.

The basic recipe couldn't be more simple:

Stir together:

unsalted peanuts

chopped nuts (e.g. Brazils, walnuts, hazelnuts, left over from Christmas)

maize

millet

currants

canary seed

sunflower seeds

ordinary bird seed

holly berries, hips and haws from the hedgerows or garden

old biscuit, bread and cake crumbs

kitchen scraps and fat – cut into fairly small pieces

cheese rind

chopped apple (you can include the peel and any bruised bits)

1 Pour melted dripping over the mixture and stir well until all the ingredients are coated (you can use cooking fat if you don't have dripping, but it must be *animal* fat and *not* vegetable fat).

2 Put the mixture into a cake tin which has a moveable bottom. Press the mixture down firmly. Put a plate with a weight on top of it and leave for at least one day.

3 Push the cake out of the tin and cut into slices as required.

P.S. If you don't have some of these ingredients you can substitute almost any kitchen scraps, but never use salted peanuts or any other salty foods, or desiccated coconut – this swells up inside the birds' stomachs.

P.P.S. The golden rule is half as much fat as your dry ingredients!!

Mini Bird Cakes

1 Make a hole in the bottom of an old yoghurt carton and push a piece of string through it. Tie a twig or an old pencil to the other end. Prepare all your cartons like this. Then fill them up with the mixture.

2 When the mixture has set hard – take the mini cakes out of the cartons and they're ready to hang on a branch or a bird table – complete with a ready made perch for the birds!

P.S. If you haven't got a bird table or a garden or a back yard – it's still worthwhile making the mixture because you can put it in an old vegetable or orange net and hang it outside on your balcony, if you live in a flat.

MIND OVER MATTER

Who doesn't like a good waterfall? It's great to get really close to one, shutting your mind to everything but the impressive roar of the water. But there's a waterfall in Wales – as beautiful as any other – that I remember for other reasons, and which I'm in no hurry to return to, at least not in the company of a man called Gary Bufton.

Gary is the leader of the Cardiff Self Defence School. They practise the martial arts of Japan, specialising in one particular form called Kyokushinkai. (No, it's not a Welsh name.) The senior members of the club, like Andrea Connery, who's the Welsh Ladies Champion, can do all those tricks like smashing tiles with one blow. But the Cardiff School have added something extra to their repertoire. It starts with a gentle jog across the Brecon Beacons.

This bit of special training only happens once a year, on the first Saturday in January, when a warm living room and the television are particularly welcoming. That's when I found myself dressed in the white Gi of the martial arts, striding out across a barren Welsh moor.

I fell in beside Andrea and

With Gary Bufton in the lead, 100 martial arts enthusiasts jogged across the Brecon Beacons.

asked her what the training was for. "It strengthens your will and determination," she replied, "It gives you discipline."

"But why do you do it?"

"Dunno really," said Andrea cheerfully, "but it's better than staying at home!"

With Gary Bufton striding out at the head of the column of more than 100 people, we soon reached the valley of the Scwyd-Yr-Eira waterfall (now that *is* a Welsh name – it means 'The Fall of the Snow') – an angry 15 metre torrent, swollen by recent rains, smashing down onto the rocks with terrific force.

And as I gazed at Scwyd-Yr-Eira, it started happening. Men and women were tearing off their clothes all around me, stripping down to the barest essentials for the main event in their afternoon's entertainment . . . a walk *under* the waterfall.

Gary was shouting orders. The whole thing was his idea. In 1976, he went to Japan and discovered that waterfall training was the ultimate test of endurance and stamina. So he brought the training back to Wales, and for the last six years, on the first Saturday in January, his pupils have been

Andrea Connery, Gary Bufton and me looking very calm *before* going under. Compare this with the next picture of me ... *after* the soaking.

Under the waterfall – the three hardy souls in the left hand corner are under the icy spray, punching and kicking the water.

making the two-mile run to the waterfall. I realised the only way to survive in the oncoming ordeal was by entering into the spirit of things as fully as possible.

So I took off my jacket, socks and trainers, and stood bare-foot on the freezing rock. My feet instantly went numb, but I decided not to worry about them. The others all seemed totally oblivious to the frost on the hillside, and they started to troop down towards the base of the waterfall, on the far side of the valley.

It might have been freezing but it made an epic sight! Over a 100 dedicated martial arts followers ranged along the valley, with the whole place echoing with the sound of the waterfall and the chants of Kyokushinkai. Then the first pair of heroes, lunatics, victims – call them whatever you like – actually went under.

The training took place on a rock ledge that jutted out under the waterfall, out of the direct flow, but well within the icy spray. I could see that the first two were soaked the instant they stood on that ledge, but they didn't even seem to notice. Instead they went through a brief routine of punches, kicks and fierce-looking grimaces and cries.

Then it was my turn. I went under with Andrea, gritting my teeth, but determined not to let cold, pain and fear overcome me. And I managed to get to the edge of the ledge and fought, really *fought* to stop my mind going blank.

Luckily, I could hear Gary yelling instructions from right behind me, so I just followed his orders.

The black belts proving they can stand anything. The rocks at the bottom were covered in ice, and they were all barefoot.

"PUNCH, PUNCH, PUNCH!!!" he shouted, so that's what I did. "Okay, that's enough," he said. I gratefully clambered down off the ledge and started looking for my towel, slightly surprised that I still had the use of my legs. 'Block of ice', 'cold as ice', 'freezing to death' – the phrase hasn't been invented to describe how I felt as I climbed out of there. *But I'd done*

it! And despite the awful cold and wet, there was this steadily-growing glow of pride and satisfaction inside me.

The training worked, I did feel more determined and stronger. Those feelings replaced the ones which told me that I and all the others were certifiably insane for doing this daft thing in the first place. I was towelling my hair as the last pair went under. People were back on the hillside now, except for a small group. These were the black belts, and Gary had a special bit saved up for them. When they'd finished paying their respects to the waterfall, they waded out into the middle of the river and, perched precariously between rocks, they trained and chanted in unison.

"Okay, boys, away you go," said Gary, and with just a touch of male arrogance they all left the river, and seemed to be saying; "Okay river, okay waterfall, we've got you under our belts, we can manage anything you can throw at us, we could stay here for *hours,* but all these other folks want to go home now." I have never seen anything so dedicated.

Later, Gary asked me if I'd be back next year. I thought about that moment of elation at having done it. I thought about the cold. I thought about my feet.

"I'll think about it," I said. But I have a feeling I'll be curled up in front of the telly while Gary, Andrea and the rest prove once again that mind can conquer matter.

This must be what a drowned rat looks like! At least it was over.

BEATRIX POTTER
IN THE LAKE DISTRICT

THE TALE OF PETER RABBIT

BEATRIX POTTER
THE ORIGINAL AND AUTHORIZED EDITION
New colour reproductions
F. WARNE & Cº

She was 27 when she wrote her first book, *The Tale of Peter Rabbit*, and *Jemima Puddle-Duck* followed soon after.

THE TALE OF JEMIMA PUDDLE-DUCK

BEATRIX POTTER
THE ORIGINAL AND AUTHORIZED EDITION
New colour reproductions
F. WARNE & Cº

The famous Rupert Potter portrait of Beatrix when she was 16 years old.

Last Spring, Goldie and I did what thousands of people do each year. We went to the Lake District, where deep lakes, like Windermere, Ullswater, Derwent and Coniston lie between the steep rocky shapes of the Lakeland Fells.

As we walked through what many people think is the most spectacular countryside in England, I said to Goldie, "Do you realise that we owe all this to Peter Rabbit, Jemima Puddle-Duck and the Flopsy Bunnies?" Goldie gave me one of her patient, long-suffering looks, but in a way, it's true.

No one could enjoy the beautiful unspoilt countryside unless someone was working hard to keep it that way. Large parts of the Lake District belong to the National Trust for Places of Natural

Beauty, and much of that land was given to them by a lady called Mrs William Heelis. Not many people (including Goldie!) know about Mrs Heelis, but when she was a little girl, her name was Beatrix Potter.

That was why Goldie and I were here, in the Lake District – to find out whatever happened to Beatrix Potter?

When she was a little girl Beatrix Potter and her brother Bertram lived a lonely life in London, with their rich stuffy parents, but every summer they escaped. Their parents rented a house in the country, and the children were free to explore a world very different from their prim nursery. Often the house was in the Lake District and for Beatrix this became a magical place of dreams and freedom.

Yet at the end of every summer she had to go back to her narrow London life, and after Bertram grew up and left home, she was lonelier than ever. She kept animals like mice and rabbits as pets, and she amused herself drawing them.

One day a little boy she knew was ill, but her parents wouldn't let her go to visit him, so she wrote him a story about four rabbits, full of drawings, to cheer him up.

Beatrix began to realise she had a gift for writing and drawing animal stories for children. She published her rabbit story, and *The Tale of Peter Rabbit* was an enormous success.

Goldie and I went to the Lake District in search of the real Beatrix Potter.

Beatrix used real places in the Lakes as settings for her books. The Tower Bank Arms at Sawrey appears in *Jemima Puddle-Duck*.

In the next few years Beatrix Potter wrote and drew many more successful books. They were all small, for children to hold, with nice clear print, and on each page wonderful coloured animal pictures. But she still lived with her parents, even though her books earned her a lot of money, and she was by now in her late thirties.

Yet every summer she still escaped to the Lake District, and one day, when she was feeling especially lonely and miserable, she saw a farm that was for sale. She made up her mind, there and then, to use some of the money from her books, and buy it for herself.

It was called Hill Top Farm! She put in a farm manager to run

George Birkett, who knew Beatrix, still breeds Herdwick sheep at High Tilberthwaite farm, as laid down in Beatrix's will.

Beatrix at 77 – bearing a remarkable resemblance to Mrs Tiggy-Winkle – with her Pekinese dog Tzusee.

does as well on all the National Trust farms as at High Tilberthwaite, it doesn't look as if Herdwick sheep are in any danger of extinction.

There are 30,000 of them today, but they might have been extinct if it hadn't been for Mrs Heelis, and as George and I strolled over his land, he told me about the rather formidable elderly lady he had known as a boy of 15.

He could remember her at the local shows and sheep sales, wearing beautifully polished black leather clogs with buckles. She won prizes – one of her best sheep was a fine ewe, called Waterlily, George recalled. She was greatly respected by the local people, which is rare for an 'off comer' to the Lake District.

When Beatrix Potter died at the age of 77, it was found that she had really left all her land to the National Trust, just as she had promised. The Trust still own her farms and care for them and the Lake District traditions just as she did, and every year thousands of walkers and holidaymakers enjoy the countryside she loved.

And 3 million Beatrix Potter books are sold every year, translated into many languages.

So the country possesses two marvellous legacies from this quiet determined woman – the unspoilt hillsides left by Mrs William Heelis, and the enchanting stories written and illustrated by Beatrix Potter!

it, and visited it whenever she could. Slowly she began to use scenes around Hill Top in her stories.

Beatrix became more and more interested in serious farming, and bought more land in the Lake District. She was helped and advised by a local solicitor, Mr William Heelis. They became close friends and then one day he asked her to marry him; so at the age of 47, Beatrix Potter became Mrs William Heelis.

Her life changed completely. She stopped writing and drawing and became a devoted farmer ready to do any job on the farm herself. The money from her books was used to buy more and more land. And William and Beatrix both agreed that when she died, she would leave it all to the National Trust.

Mrs Heelis particularly loved the sturdy sheep that grazed on the Lakeland slopes of her farms. They're called Herdwicks – Beatrix liked their rugged strength that helped them withstand the bitter winters. She laid down that after she died, the National Trust must still breed Herdwicks on her farms, like High Tilberthwaite Farm near Coniston.

George Birkett and his family run the farm now, and I joined him while his Herdwicks were lambing. He had brought the flock down from the High Fells so that he could keep an eye on them, and it was fascinating to see the ewes with their lambs – the lambs are born black, but they soon change to dark grey, and then lighter grey as they get older.

I gave George a hand while one lamb was being born. It was soon feeding so eagerly that if lambing

There are 30,000 Herdwicks today which might have been extinct if it wasn't for Beatrix and George.

Underwater Pop Concert

Richard Kelly is the director who does all the really weird films. Remember when we went to Bath to take the waters? That was Richard Kelly. He also has a very wicked sense of humour, so when he asked if I'd like to go to an Underwater Pop Concert, I tried to think of a smart answer, like "OK, but after we've been to the Free-fall Opera." But he was serious.

When I was told I was going to an Underwater Pop Concert at Liverpool University, I thought it was a hoax, but it turned out to be true.

It began as a serious experiment. If dolphins make musical noises underwater, would they enjoy rock music played to them through a special underwater speaker?

The students at Liverpool University had become very interested in the possibility of sound travelling underwater. Whales and dolphins for instance, wouldn't survive if they couldn't make sounds underwater because they use them to hunt for food. The noises they make bounce back from the thing they're after, which tells them how far away it is. Their delicate built-in echo-finders make them very sensitive to sound patterns, so there was the possibility that they would like music if they could hear it under water.

The answer was 'no'. They hated it and shot off to the other side of the pool, but when we tried opera they loved it.

To find out, Steve Millard and I dived into a Dolphinarium to meet two friendly dolphins called Clive and Sooty. We took with us a specially designed speaker that actually works underwater. The first piece of entertainment was a blast of rock music to shatter their bubbling tranquillity.

They hated it!

You couldn't see their flippers for bubbles as they shot off to the other side of the pool as far away from the underwater speakers as possible.

Our next number was a bit more upmarket, 'Oh My Beloved Daddy' from an opera by Puccini.

It knocked them out!

They came gliding across from the other side of the pool, dipping and swirling around us to the music. Quite seriously Clive and Sooty seemed positively to enjoy the opera, as much as they hated the rock music. They both appeared to match their body movements to the music and they looked quite crestfallen when we climbed out of the water.

Meanwhile at the University things at the swimming pool were really hotting up as the guests began to arrive for the Underwater Pop Concert. The first person to take to the waters was a Bishop complete with crozier and underwater mitre. Next came Kermit the Frog who was more appropriately dressed, although I *did* wonder about the lady with the black stockings and frilly petticoats.

After playing human music to the dolphins we tried to play whale music to the humans. Whales make a very distinct and quite musical sound underwater. This was relayed to the submerged audience by special underwater speakers. Immediately 2 deaf students bobbed to the surface to tell their teacher with great excitement, that they had heard a little of the sound, and had definitely felt the vibrations.

By now the band had arrived. They played in the dry, but the sound was relayed to the audience on the bottom of the pool. Marina Morena had come all the way from Venezuela to sing "Summer Time", which suited the underwater acoustics perfectly.

The concert finished with a rave-up to the rock music that the dolphins Clive and Sooty found so objectionable. The students loved it. The atmosphere on the bottom of the pool was like 'Top of the Pops' with the music in real time but the dancing at quarter speed – with bubbles.

On the way back to London in the train I told Richard Kelly how much I'd enjoyed it all.

"There you are, you see, you didn't believe me, did you?"

Well, perhaps I had been a bit sceptical.

After a long pause he said, "Do you really think we could do a free-fall opera?"

I looked through the window and pretended not to hear. I thought it was best.

. . . But the real party was going on at the bottom of the pool as I joined the students to rock the night away.

KERMIT'S

My eyes were not deceiving me – this *was* a real, live, yellow frog!

Remember when the world's most famous frog brought Jim Henson to the studio? Bonnie and Willow certainly won't forget Kermit in a hurry! They couldn't make head or tail of the frisky green frog with the big red mouth and shot off out of his way – which is why they're not in this photo! But even more baffling were the frogs Mr Ibbotson found in his garden – they were red, yellow and *real!*

Mr Ibbotson hasn't a clue why his flowers and veg have coloured frogs hopping in and out of them. They've made their home in his Wheathampstead garden for 16 years now and apart from their colour, they seem perfectly normal.

Our pond expert Brian Banks says frogs do vary in colour because they tend to camouflage themselves, according to the colour of the foliage that surrounds them. But Mr Ibbotson says he doesn't have any yellow or orange flowers in his garden! *He* thinks his frogs may look so extraordinary as a result of the weed killer, a nearby farmer sprays on his crops – if that's true, it doesn't seem to have done them any harm.

You'd think that brightly coloured frogs would be spotted by predators like birds, cats, dogs or rats. But Mr Ibbotson thinks they've survived because they're very timid. He's keen to hear from anyone else with coloured frogs like his, so if you know of any near your home, drop us a line and we'll pass it on to him.

But there's no mystery about the frogs or the newts in our garden at Television Centre. It's a seething mass of them – and as they've all

56

COUSINS

been bred in our wildlife pond, we're very proud of our efforts on behalf of conservation. Frogs are the gardener's friend – they polish off the slugs more efficiently than any poisons and the more there are, the better.

Last autumn, Brian Banks took us on the Great Frog and Newt Hunt. It wasn't a long safari – just a few metres across the Blue Peter garden – because the babies had hopped to some very strange places. They weren't sheltering amongst the grass or leaves, as you might expect. They'd made for a huge piece of board we keep next to the greenhouse, to stop the cameras sinking into the ground, when we're filming in there with

Percy.

It was quite a tense moment before we lifted the board. "You'll have to be quick," warned Brian. "They're the same colour as the earth, so it's hard to see them, and they move like lightning."

"Got you!" yelled Peter, as he spotted a really tiddly frog and popped it in a large glass jar.

"Look at this!" I couldn't believe my eyes – I'd spotted a tiny smooth newt – next there was a Palamate just about to wriggle under a stone. Our jars were filling up, which was good, because Brian said the tiny creatures would only get squashed, if we left them under the board.

We released the babies near some large stones and shady plants.

It was very satisfying to think we'd bred two generations of amphibians – not bad for a tiny

home-made wildlife pond, in the heart of a big city.

By the time this book is published, with David Bellamy's help, we'll have built a complete Wildlife Garden on some wasteland by the side of Television Centre. And our ambition is to try and breed a really rare amphibian – the Great Crested Newt. And if we succeed – there's no reason why *you* shouldn't either. Every tadpole that hatches into a frog – every flower that feeds a butterfly or a bee helps to protect our vanishing wildlife. I bet Kermit would approve!

The greatest treasure trove from the depths of the ocean – £10,000,000 – and that was just the ballast!

THE NANKING CARGO

Captain Hatcher, a diver and everyone's idea of a swashbuckling adventurer, came to the Blue Peter studio to tell us about his amazing discovery.

Blue Peter

The valuable cargo on board the Dutch Merchantman when she set sail from the port of Nanking in China bound for Amsterdam, was tea. Because 200 years ago tea was a great delicacy that only the very rich could afford. Tea is quite light, as cargoes go, so the Dutch traders packed a load of porcelain underneath the tea. This gave ballast to the ship, and the tea gave protection to the china. No flies on the Dutch master or on the Chinese dockworkers who loaded the cargo.

But they were never to know the full extent of their cleverness.

A typhoon, the scourge of the South China Sea, blew up. The ship went down with all hands. It has lain on the bottom of the ocean for 234 years.

Then enter Mike Hatcher, who looks like everyone's dream of a swashbuckling adventurer, and his diving team.

Captain Hatcher knew there was a wreck down there somewhere, but he had no idea what was on board. They searched for over a year but found nothing. They all decided to dive for two more days, and then give up and go home.

On the second day – the last day – they found a gun, and then, the anchor. And as one of the divers looked closely at the sea bed, he saw pieces of broken plates!

They dug into the sand, and parts of the wreckage began to emerge.

Then, suddenly – a blackout!

A swirling mass of inky water totally destroyed the divers' vision.

It was tea!

At first they thought they had spent all that time and money just to find a load of 200 year old tea. But as they scraped and blew it away, rows and rows of china bowls began to appear through

One day the voice of a diver broke through on the radio to the crew on deck: "Surface – Surface – I've discovered gold!"

the blackness. Not ruined and barnacle encrusted, but gleaming and looking just as new as the day they were packed two centuries ago. In another part of the ship they discovered a dish that had not been protected by the tea, and that was covered in barnacles and had lost all its sheen.

The team worked on.

"It was not long before we all started to curse the very thing that had protected the treasure!" said Captain Hatcher. "It produced the worst diving conditions I have ever experienced. Once you started to blow with the compressed air, it was like swimming in a teapot! It was everywhere, it stank, and every time the diver sucked he got a putrid mouthful. It invaded all the equipment and we had to keep surfacing to clean out all the pipes

Hidden beneath a cargo of tea at the bottom of the South China Sea for more than 200 years was a priceless collection of china.

and joints. And visibility was absolutely nil!"

They managed to get the china, all 168,000 pieces of it, aboard their ship. It was cleaned as it was brought to the surface, and Captain Hatcher and his crew began to realise the splendour of their discovery.

Beautiful blue and white china porcelain, thousands of plates, dishes, cups and saucers, all destined for the dining tables of Europe – there was even a load of chamber pots, destined to go under the finest beds in Europe!

The treasure belonged to the Dutch government, because the ship was a Dutch merchantman, but Captain Hatcher and his crew were entitled to treasure trove, a reward for finding the cargo.

But fortune had one more ace to play them!

Captain Hatcher told us, "I remember one day about half a dozen of us were sitting on the deck having a cup of tea, when the diver broke in on the radio:

Surface – Surface.

I'VE DISCOVERED **GOLD!**"

Those are the words every diver dreams of hearing.

Within minutes the diver was on deck, falling over from the weight of a stack of gold bars.

"We all cheered and whooped for sheer joy!"

There were 125 gold ingots in all, and it was to be the first time that 18 carat Chinese gold had been seen in the West.

Blue Peter was lucky, too, to be the first television programme to show some of the exhibits from the Nanking Cargo.

But meeting Captain Hatcher was almost as big a thrill as seeing the cargo. He is a tall, well-built man, with a charming smile, and a trace of an Australian accent.

He has spent many years in Australia, but he was born in York, and was brought up in a

Dr Barnardo's Home. He has the happiest memories of Dr Barnardo's, and is still in touch with the friends he made there.

He intends to spend part of his treasure trove reward on founding a scholarship to help today's Barnardo's boys and girls with their further education.

It is nice to think that there are boys and girls at Barnardo's whose future will be made rosier because of the cargo that left Nanking in 1752 – and didn't land in Amsterdam until 1986!

It was tea that preserved the china from being ruined by the sea. This is what happened to a pot stored on deck which did not have the protection of the tea.

Snug in a SNOOD

You don't need a fortune to keep the Winter winds at bay with a high fashion headwarmer like one of these.

A 100g pack of stockingette roll, from a supermarket or car-care shop costs under £1 and makes a snood or a scarf.

You can use the stockingette plain or dyed to any colour you like. But wash it well first. The hottest washing machine wash is ideal, or soak it overnight with soap powder and then rinse well.

If you want to colour it to match your outfit, use a cold water dye, and follow the manufacturers instructions carefully.

To make the simplest snood, that covers both your head and neck, pull the tube of material inside itself to make a double-thickness.

Pull the raw edges over your head down to your neck, and let the folded edge frame your face. Arrange the spare material in folds around your neck, and tuck the raw edges inside.

For a turban effect, leave the material as a single-thickness. Just fold in the raw edge to neaten it and put it over your head with the folded edge framing your face (like putting on a bobble hat). Take the long end hanging down at the back or side, and wind it round your head, tucking in the ends.

To vary the style, leave some of the length of material hanging out like a tail. Tie the end in a knot to hide the raw edges – this gives a pirate cap effect.

If you want to dye a second batch of material, you can use the dye again to get a paler shade of the same colour. Twist this second piece of material around your first snood for yet another style! And to make a scarf – use a length of the material and knot the ends.

PUSSY WILLOW

Birthday
11th May 1986

Breed
Balinese Varient

Mother
Blue Point Siamese

Father
Balinese
(a long haired Siamese)

Eyes
Blue

Colour when born
Pure White

Colour now
Smoky brown

First Blue Peter Appearance
11th September 1986

Habits
Retrieves twists of newspaper,
like a dog. Collects toys and puts
them in piles under chairs

Favourite Food
Cream cheese

Likes
All dogs

Dislikes
Milk

Fire At York

2.30 a.m. Monday 9th July 1984: A sultry night in York. A bolt of lightning strikes the South Transept of York Minster and sets fire to the massive, dry beams in the Transept's roof. The York skyline is lit up as the fire spreads and people watch fearfully as 900 years of history threatens to vanish before their eyes.

Dawn: the fire is being damped down, most of the Minster has escaped, but the South Transept, home of the glorious Rose Window, is destroyed, the roof timbers have fallen and 68 bosses – the lynchpins in the ceiling structure – lie smouldering on the floor . . .

Friday 16th May 1986: Rebuilding has been going on since the day of the fire. The new roof beams have been fixed into place. Modern technology has been combined with age-old crafts to restore the Rose Window and create a new South Transept. The banging and hammering stops for a few minutes as the first of the new decorative bosses is hoisted into the ceiling. It shows the Tudor Rose, symbol of the Rose Window, coming through a surround of flames. As it makes the long journey up into the roof, you can just read the name of the artist on the side . . . Laura E. J. Smith.

The boss was designed by ten year old Laura, and five more also designed by Blue Peter viewers, were chosen as the result of one of the most successful competitions we've ever held. When we were asked by the Dean of York, the Very Reverend John Southgate, to see if our viewers could come up with six ideas for replacement bosses. We never dreamed we'd get so many imaginative and brilliant suggestions.

We asked viewers for ideas for the new bosses showing important happenings this century, that they'd like people to remember 1000 years from now.

32,373 people sent us sketches and drawings. The most popular themes were space and Concorde. Other ideas showed peace between nations showing doves and clasped hands; conservation with pandas, whales and plant life; Live Aid and Ethiopia; the Minster on fire; the *Mary Rose*; the Channel Tunnel and transport through the century.

2000 runners-up were awarded what is, without

The six winners used binoculars – part of their prize – to examine the bosses in the ceiling.

The North Transept, which escaped the flames. Where each supporting arch in the ceiling meets, there's a boss acting as a keystone, helping to hold the structure together and adding decoration to the Minster.

We showed 2,000 entries in the studio – all by runners up.

The six winners and their winning designs. There's a carved, unpainted boss there too.

Simon saw how the glaziers restored the scorched and cracked Rose Window. Advanced technology and ancient skills were both needed to do the repairs.

doubt, the most unusual prize we've ever stuffed into an envelope . . . little chunks of burnt wood! They were fragments from the burned South Transept roof, branded with the York Minster shield and our Blue Peter ship.

The six top winners each received a pair of binoculars – very useful to see all the detail inside the cathedral – and the grandest prize of all: their designs would be turned into carved, painted bosses by the craftsmen at York, and fixed into the ceiling where, with luck, they should remain for centuries.

But the competition didn't end with the announcement of the results. Simon took the six winners to York a few weeks later, so they could meet Geoff Butler and Nick Quayle, the carvers who were going to create the new bosses. Geoff and Nick have carved most of the new bosses. Their designs were based mainly on the words

Rebecca-Rose Welsh, who drew the 'Spaceman on the Moon' design, explained to Nick Quayle how he should turn her picture into a carved boss.

Simon standing *above* the repaired South Transept ceiling. The weather proof covering is where the new roof will be eventually.

of a psalm, so the Blue Peter bosses will certainly stand out.

The six winners explained to Geoff and Nick how they wanted their designs to look.

"It would be good if you could get the hands into more of a cup-shape," said Tim Hutchinson, the oldest of the winners, whose theme was 'Famine Relief'.

"How would you like the flames?" Geoff asked Laura Smith, "on the top of the boss, or going right round the sides?"

The carvers also knew what was possible, and what was not.

"I don't think I can get all the detail on that rigging," said Nick, "anyway, I don't think it'll show up when it's seen from down on the ground."

"That's alright," said Joanna Biggs who designed the *'Mary Rose* Raised from the Sea', "but perhaps you can make the ship stand out more."

"What's in his pocket?" said Nick to six year old Rebecca-Rose Welsh, looking at her 'Spaceman on the Moon'.

"His sandwiches!" replied Rebecca-Rose.

The carving took weeks of skilled work, and even more weeks for the painting to be done. We itched to go back to York to see how the work was coming on.

Eventually, the first two bosses were ready and all the winners were back at the Minster to see how they'd turned out. None of us will ever forget the first sight of a finished Blue Peter boss. It was Richard Gaston's marine conservation design a 'Diver and the Whale'. The blue, green and silver shone out and the intricate carving had been done brilliantly. A real work of art had been created by the combined efforts of Richard and the York craftsmen.

It seemed incredible that the metre-wide, roughly hewn, half-spheres of oak had been transformed into such delicate and moving images. It was marvellous to see them close-up, and yet the carvers and painters had been so skilled with their use of shapes and colours that there can't be any doubt that the bosses will also show up well when future visitors to the Minster see them from 30 metres below – standing on the South Transept floor.

And then came that great moment, when we fixed the chains to Laura's boss and the pulleys hoisted it up, high into the new South Transept roof. Who didn't have a tear in their eyes as the design which, more than any other, symbolises the survival of Minster, made its final journey, up and up, into the forest of beams. What a stirring and awesome thought that generations of people in hundreds of years time look up at that boss, and wonder about the

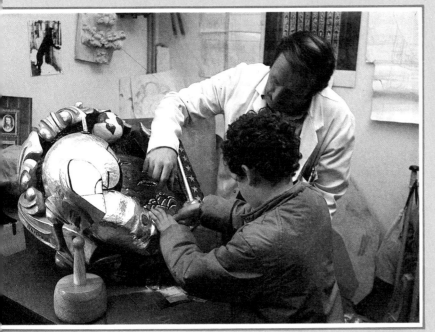

Ben Kerslake applying silver leaf to his boss, 'Neil Armstrong on the Moon', under the guidance of Geoff Butler.

Competition Winners

Laura Smith and her 'Rose Window Coming Through the Flames'

Tim Hutchinson's 'Famine Relief' design

Rebecca-Rose Welsh's 'Spaceman on the Moon'

Richard Gaston's 'Diver and Whale'

The magic moment! The first Blue Peter boss on its long journey up to the new ceiling.

Laura watches as the workmen bolt 'The Rose Window Coming through the Flames', into position.

Ben Kerslake's 'Neil Armstrong on the Moon'

people who created it and the time they lived in. And if they read about the tragic fire, perhaps they will also learn about the six children whose ideas and designs were chosen to represent our century. Let's hope they do, and let's hope the Minster stands for another 900 years!

STOP PRESS! It's expected that the huge rebuilding work will finally be completed by the end of 1988 and that the new South Transept will be opened to the public. If you go along, don't forget to take your binoculars!

Joanna Biggs designed 'The Mary Rose Raised from the Sea'

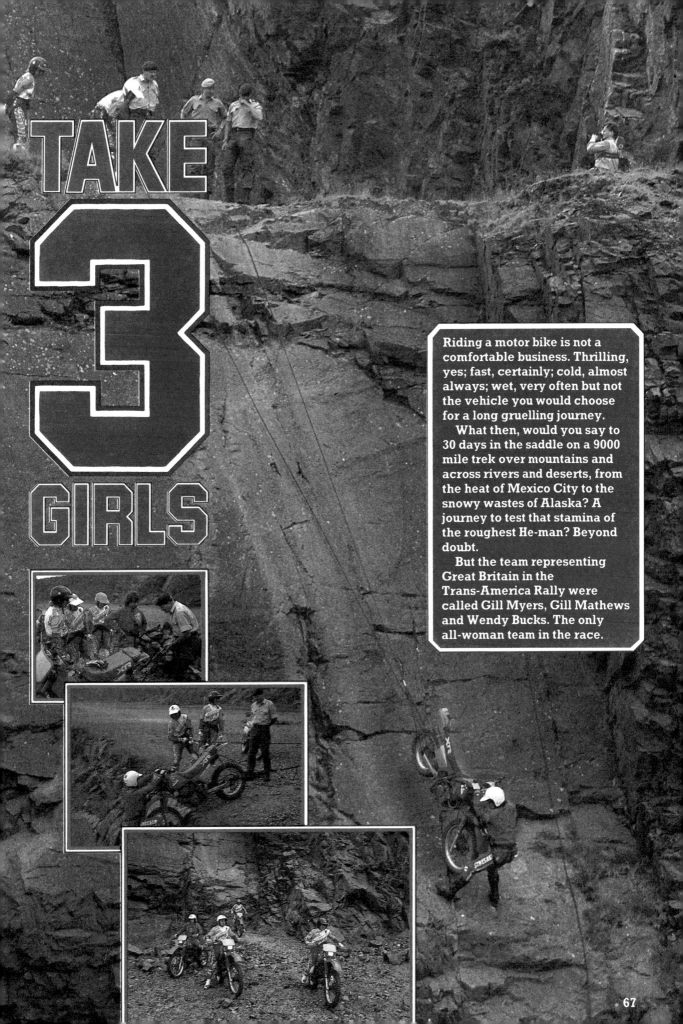

TAKE 3 GIRLS

Riding a motor bike is not a comfortable business. Thrilling, yes; fast, certainly; cold, almost always; wet, very often but not the vehicle you would choose for a long gruelling journey.

What then, would you say to 30 days in the saddle on a 9000 mile trek over mountains and across rivers and deserts, from the heat of Mexico City to the snowy wastes of Alaska? A journey to test that stamina of the roughest He-man? Beyond doubt.

But the team representing Great Britain in the Trans-America Rally were called Gill Myers, Gill Mathews and Wendy Bucks. The only all-woman team in the race.

I had a camera fitted to my helmet, so that *you* could experience the thrill of the ride with me.

I joined them for a training session on Dartmoor with a borrowed bike and a little help from the Royal Marines. That part of Devonshire is pretty rugged and provided some of the obstacles the girls would find in their race across America.

We rough rode along stony pot-holed tracks and across the wild open terrain of the moor. I'd had a little biking experience with the famous White Helmets display team, so I was feeling quite confident as I rode behind the

We had to dismantle all four bikes and load them on to the inflatable.

When the girls get to America they will have to cross rivers far wider than the Tamar.

Walking backwards pulling a motorbike down a vertical cliff is every bit as difficult as it looks!

shower of mud that I believed to be Wendy. Then, quite suddenly the mud shower disappeared, and so did Wendy.

The next second I was over the handlebars and head first into the middle of a bog. But I was no longer alone. Beside me was Wendy, up to her neck in mud and laughing like a drain. Manhandling the bikes out of the mud was an important test of how fast the girls could recover from a disaster and be back in the race again.

How do you drive a bike over a cliff? And survive? Answer: send for the Royal Marines. Sergeant Dave Stocks and his team showed us how to abseil down a cliff. Not all that difficult, I hear you say.

But towing a 250cc motor bike behind you?

If the front wheel slipped over (and it did!) there was a distinct danger of the bike slicing the legs from under you. After a few hair-raising moments all three girls, four bikes and me were back on terra firma, and roaring off across the moor again.

Ordeal by water was the next test. The girls will have to cross some huge rivers in America, so with some advice from Sergeant Taff Summers and the men of 539 Assault Squadron, we faced the waters of the Tamar. The Marines lent us a large inflatable, but not big enough to take us *and* the four bikes. There was only one thing

We made it to the other side. Now we only had one small problem. How to put the bikes together again!

for it. Every bike would have to come to pieces. We set to with screwdrivers and spanners, loading the bits into the boat in reverse order so that we would re-assemble them faster when we got to the other side. Some of the parts were extremely heavy. The biggest bit of all, the frame, needed all four of us to hump it into the boat.

By the time we were all embarked there was a strong tide running and it needed a huge effort on the paddles to stop us from drifting upstream, but we made it. Now there was only one small problem. How to get the four bikes back together again.

Destruction is always easier then construction, and with that in mind I had carefully put every nut and screw and bolt into a large plastic bag, because the loss of one small part could leave us with a pile of scrap instead of a running motor bike. In the end I found that I had four completely re-assembled motor bikes,and a handful of nuts left over! But the bikes didn't seem to mind, so I gave up worrying and roared off after the girls.

It had been a tough, but very exciting day and I was left feeling quite humbled by the rugged determination of those three girls. The other 30 competing countries had better watch out, because if sheer guts, a sense of humour and team work have anything to do with it, our girls are in with a shout.

THE VILLAGE LOST IN TIME

The Story of the Cropthorne Camera

Last summer I stood in the centre of a quiet country village in the heart of the Worcester countryside. The village was called Cropthorne. I was at the end of the most extraordinary detective story I had ever heard.

It all began 180 miles away, in Plymouth, when one afternoon Colin Webb, a local teacher, went browsing round the antique shops and junk stores on the sea front, hoping to pick up an odd bargain.

He came upon an old wooden box, and when he opened it, he found it was full of glass slides. Most people would have made nothing of them, but Colin was a keen amateur photographer and he knew at once they were glass negatives from the very early days of photography.

Very excited, he bought the lot for five pounds, and took them home. There he spent agonising hours in his dark room, until gradually, one by one, images began to appear through the developing liquid.

There was a man in country clothes with his dog and carrying

Colin Webb found some old glass negatives in a junk shop. They were pictures of a village. But not until he enlarged this section of a picture, did he discover the village's identity.

Retracing Colin's steps I found that Cropthorne still looked like those old pictures.

This is one of the pictures taken 100 years ago . . .

. . . And this one was taken last summer of Goldie and me, with a camera just like the one used to shoot the original – you can see how little has changed.

This is Minnie Holland – the mystery photographer. Minnie was the daughter of the local squire.

CROPTHORNE POST OFFICE

The main street of Cropthorne as Minnie saw it . . .

. . . And with the camera in the same position this is how Goldie and I saw it 100 years later.

a shot gun – and a main village street, lined with trees. There were boarded cottages with thatched roofs – and a group of villagers outside a shop, with children playing.

Colin was watching the first pictures of a village and its people emerge from the negatives of 100 years ago. He was uncovering a village lost in time! But what village could it possibly be? There was just one clue. In one of the pictures a half-timbered house had a sign over the door, but it was too small to read.

Back to the dark room again, where Colin enlarged that part of the photograph, until he could just make out the words:

THAT was the name of the village!

He looked through maps and road atlases until he found it – a few dots on the map between Pershore and Evesham, in Worcestershire.

When I went to Cropthorne, I began to relive the excitement Colin felt as he made his first visit there!

On his journey from Plymouth he must have wondered if it had totally changed.

But to his delight and surprise, he found that he recognised the village immediately! The very same streets and houses that had been photographed 100 years ago were still standing. Even the old Post Office with the vital clue, was still there, although it had become a private house now.

He was in a time warp. The scenes – that perfectly matched the black and white photos – were almost unaltered by the passage of time. But who had taken the original pictures?

Colin met an old lady called Mrs Cornell, who had lived in Cropthorne all her life. She knew the name of the photographer of 100 years ago. It was Minnie

Holland. Her father was the local squire, who owned the biggest house in the district, and most of the village of Cropthorne. In those days it was unthinkable that a young lady should work for a living, they taught in the Sunday School, or sang in the church choir, or had hobbies. Minnie's hobby was photography. She must have caused quite a stir as she lugged her huge plate camera through the village streets. Minnie bought prepared glass negatives, and loaded her camera with them one at a time – rolls of film were not invented till years later!

Then she developed the plates herself, in a little room at Cropthorne Court, that she had made into a dark room.

Glass negatives needed a long exposure, which is why Minnie liked taking pictures of buildings, because they couldn't move. And of course, the villagers and their children were so much in awe of the Squire's daughter, they would sit absolutely still for hours if she wanted to take their picture.

One of the little girls in the picture was called Kitty Hyde, Mrs Cornell remembered. When she grew up, she went away and trained as a teacher. Then she came back to Cropthorne and was the village schoolmistress for 42 years.

I was able to meet Mrs Rose Cornell, the elderly lady who told Colin Webb all about Minnie Holland, for myself. She is very frail now and lives at Evesham Hospital, but she was strong enough to point out some of her own family who lived in Cropthorne when Minnie Holland was taking her remarkable pictures.

Minnie was very clever, Mrs Cornell told me, but she never

It was an old lady called Mrs Cornell who first told Colin the name of the photographer, so Goldie and I went to see her.

She remembered Minnie and was able to pick out people who were featured in the original photographs.

. . . Some of them were from Mrs Cornell's own family.

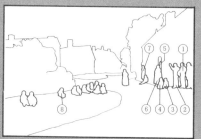

1 Father: Charlie Meakin
2 Uncle Peter
3 Elder sister: Lizzie Meakin
4 Elder brother: Jim Meakin
5 Mother: Laura Meakin
6 Grandmother: Ann Taylee
7 Godmother: (Eliza Rose?)
8 Younger brother: Hubert

married. In fact, of all Squire Holland's seven children, only two married, and only one had a child, a daughter. She lived near Plymouth, and when her Aunt

Minnie died, she took over her things – so that explains why the pictures from Cropthorne were found 180 miles away in Plymouth.

There is just one picture that has survived of Minnie Holland. For years she was almost forgotten. Yet now, the Holland family, Cropthorne, and the village people will always be remembered – thanks to Minnie Holland and the Cropthorne camera, and Colin Webb's amazing detective work!

And it made me wonder what other treasures there are, hidden in attics and old boxes, or pushed into bookshelves – all waiting to be discovered.

UP HELLY AA!!

Dear Mark,
Every year on the last Tuesday of January we have a Viking Festival called Up-Helly-Aa. One man for one night has control of the streets of Lerwick. We call this man the Guizer Jarl (pronounced Yarl) and this year my father has the chance of a lifetime to be the Jarl.

Will you come to the Shetlands and film Up-Helly-Aa?
Yours sincerely,
Rae Simpson

So off I went, hotfoot to the Shetland Islands.

The Shetlands are steeped in Viking traditions and Up-Helly-Aa is the most famous of them. The centre-piece of Up-Helly-Aa is the burning of a Viking galley but it's only one part of a hugely complex organization that begins months before. The Guizer Jarl, which roughly translates to 'Chief Actor', is the man in charge of the proceedings. That's the position of honour held by Rae's father, Magnus Simpson.

I met Magnus and Rae on the morning of Up-Helly-Aa, and the Viking galley was being moved from its shed into public view for the first and only time. Decorated with white painted Viking shields *Sungam*, the Viking galley, was built according to tradition – 11 oars and shields on each side, the hull 10 metres long and the dragon's head four and a half metres tall.

she looked brilliant even in the overcast Shetland dawn.

The longship's destiny is to be burned on Up-Helly-Aa night. She goes up in a crackling, violent blaze in the same way that longships did when they were used for funerals of chieftains in Viking times. This is the tradition that is recalled on Up-Helly-Aa.

It's the Guizer Jarl's right to name his galley, and Magnus

chose *Sungam* – Magnus spelt backwards!

Large groups of men accompanied *Sungam* on her march round Lerwick. They were organized into groups called 'Guizing Squads'. The most important of these was the Guizer Jarl's Squad, all dressed like the Jarl himself, in glittering silver Viking armour and wearing sheepskin cloaks and winged helmets. Most of them had beards as well, so they made a fearsome sight.

I had to watch the procession, rather than march in it, because no outsiders can take part in Up-Helly-Aa. However, I was able to dress up as a Viking to take part in the Junior Up-Helly-Aa. The children had a small longship, and with great festivity, we carted that around the town and up it went in a very satisfying cloud of smoke.

Sungam spent most of the day on the harbour side and by that evening she was ready for her last voyage. Accompanied by the Lerwick Brass Band, the Guizers created the scene that has made the Shetlands famous. Each man was carrying a flaming torch, and 800 of them lit up the night sky. Magnus leapt up onto *Sungam*

and the procession was off. It wound its way round Lerwick again, the band playing for all they were worth, the Guizers singing their hearts out. The doubled ranks of flaming torches stretched back almost 500 metres at one point in the march.

At the Burning Site, *Sungam* was removed from her trailer. The crowd of torches around her got larger and larger, showing that nearly all the Guizers had arrived. I could just see Magnus through all the sparks, still standing on the longship. When I saw him climb down, I knew the highlight of the celebration had arrived.

There was a blast from the band – the signal for the burning to begin. Under a torrent of flaming torches, *Sungam* virtually disappeared behind the flames. Just the top of the mast remained visible, until that too crashed to the ground. And while the burning reached its height, the Guizers

The majesty of Up-Helly-Aa – the torchlit procession snakes through Lerwick towards the climax of the celebration.

sang the anthem of Up-Helly-Aa, 'The Norseman's Home'.

"Then let us ne'er forget the race
Who bravely fought and died
Who never filled a craven's grave
But ruled the foaming tide."

That was just the start of the evening, and what followed was just as enjoyable. 13 halls around Lerwick stayed open all night, to greet each of the Guizer Squads. There was much singing and dancing and I had a marvellous time, taking advantage of some of the warmest hospitality you're ever likely to meet. It went on till past four o'clock. So if you want a good sleep, don't go anywhere near Lerwick on the last Tuesday in January!

The procession organized by the local school children also made an impressive sight. Can you spot the Viking with glasses?

The height of the blaze – *Sungam* the Viking galley is consumed in flames. 20 metres away, I could still feel the heat!

Solutions

Now find a mirror

Puzzle Pictures

1 Sculptor **David Peterson** created these life-like pink flamingoes.

2 **Stan Laurel** and **Oliver Hardy** bearing a remarkable resemblance to Roy Castle and Janet Ellis, celebrating the **50th anniversary** of the first Stan and Ollie film.

3 The remote controlled bathroom of the future – you can turn on the taps when you're lying in bed!

4 **Giants of Land and Sea!** Some of the colossal creatures used to launch our **Natural History Museum** competition.

5 12 year old **Robert Goaman** covered in soot after rescuing his cat, **Barney**, who had spent seven days down the chimney.

6 **Paul Daniels** came to meet 15 year old **Roy Davenport** who won the British Magician's Grand Prix, competing with magicians three times his age.

7 Acrobats from the **Peking Opera** who gave a dazzling display in the Blue Peter studio.

8 The two miniature jet planes designed to be driven like cars.

9 A **Time Machine** designed by **William Longden** for the children of Henry Fawcett's Infants School.

10 The gravity-defying exercise machine that is being tested by students at the **West London Institute of Higher Education** may be of great help to handicapped and disabled people.

11 Face to face with **Sil** from **Dr. Who**.

How to win a Blue Peter Badge!

We award Blue Peter badges for interesting letters, good ideas for the programme, stories, poems, drawings, paintings and for models that have been particularly well made. There are four badges – Blue, Silver, Gold and Competition. To win a Silver badge you have to do something different from your Blue badge project.

For instance, if you won a Blue badge for an interesting letter, you could win a Silver one by sending us a good idea for the programme, or a painting, or a model.

Gold badges are only awarded for really outstanding achievements – for instance, saving somebody's life or representing your country in an international sporting event. Competition badges are awarded to winners of Blue Peter competitions.

There are over 50 Museums, Exhibitions and other important places of interest to which your Blue Peter badge guarantees that you will be admitted free of charge. If you are already a badge winner, and would like a free admission list up-date, send a stamped addressed envelope to the Blue Peter office, BBC TV Centre, London W12 7RJ.

Useful Information

Royal Commonwealth Society for the Blind
Commonwealth House, Haywards Heath, West Sussex. RH16 3AZ. Tel: 0444 412424

Cardiff School of Self Defence
58-60 Salisbury Road, Cathays, Cardiff. CF2 4AA. Tel: 0222 24350

Beatrix Potter's Farm
Hill Top, Near Sawrey, Ambleside. LA22 0LF. Tel: 096 66269

Beatrix Potter: Artist, storyteller and Countrywoman
by Judy Taylor, Published by Frederick Warne. Price: £12.95

The National Shire Horse Centre
Dunstone, Yealmpton, Plymouth, Devon. PL8 2EL. Tel: 0752 880806

Young Ornithologists' Club
The Lodge, Sandy, Bedfordshire. SG19 2DL. Tel: 0767 80551

Auto Cycle Union
Miller House, Corporation Street, Rugby, Warwickshire. CV21 2DN Tel: 0788 70332

The Nanking Cargo
by Michael Hatcher with Antony Thorncroft, Published by Hamish Hamilton. Price: £12.95

Acknowledgements
Co-ordinator: Anne Dixon
Designed by: Ray Hyden and Adrian Calder
Typeset by: Type Generation

Peach Melba, The Grand Tour and **Beatrix Potter in the Lake District** were written by Dorothy Smith.
A Village Lost In Time was retold by **Dorothy Smith** from the book 'Minnie Holland's Camera 1892-1905' by E R Cornell, G H Keating and C D Webb, published by Kawabata Press, Knill Cross House, Knill Cross, Millbrook, Nr. Torpoint, Cornwall
The Grand Tour and **Peach Melba** were illustrated by **Robert Broomfield.**

Cress Heads and Snoods by **Margaret Parnell.**

Photographs were taken by **Joan Williams, Robert Hill, Barry Boxall, Chris Capstick, John Jefford, Conrad Hafenrichter,** **Sally Humphries, Alex Leger** and **Michael Cook** with the exception of Nellie Melba archive photograph p 9 Performing Arts Museum, p10 by BBC Hulton Picture Library, Culver Pictures Inc., New York; Birds' Banquet photographs p 46 by RSPB; Beatrix Potter photograph pp 51-53 by R S Hart; front cover of *The Tale of Peter Rabbit* by Beatrix Potter (Frederick Warne & Co., 1902), copyright © Frederick Warne & Co., 1902, 1987; front cover of *The Tale Of Jemima Puddle-Duck* by Beatrix Potter (Frederick Warne & Co., 1908), copyright © Frederick Warne & Co., 1908, 1987; two illustrations from *The Tale Of Jemima Puddle-Duck* by Beatrix Potter (Frederick Warne & Co., 1908), copyright © Frederick Warne & Co., 1908, p.44; Nanking Cargo photographs pp 58-60 by Christie's; York Minster photograph p 63 by Woodmansterne/Hilton-Scott; The Village Lost in Time photographs pp 70-72 by Kawabata Press; pp39 Helmet photograph; Sotheby's.

Blue Peter

COMPETITION

Would you like to come to TV Centre and meet us and, Bonnie and Willow? This could be your chance to come to London and meet us all at a special party – and see the Blue Peter studio!

JANET'S JUMP

Janet spent three years training for her record breaking Free Fall (interrupted by breaking her pelvis!). Altogether she made 33 practice jumps. If all these were added together – *including her final Free Fall* – how many feet has Janet jumped altogether? Work out your answer and fill in the entry form on this page.

The people who come up with the estimates nearest the correct figure will be invited to our **Blue Peter Party!** And there'll be lots of Competition badges for the Runners-Up, too!

Send your entry to:
**Blue Peter,
Janet's Jump Competition,
BBC TV Centre,
London W12 7RJ.**

The closing date for entries is the **13th January 1988**. The First Prize Winners and Runners-Up will be notified by letter.

feet

Janet has jumped

Name......................

Address......................

Age............

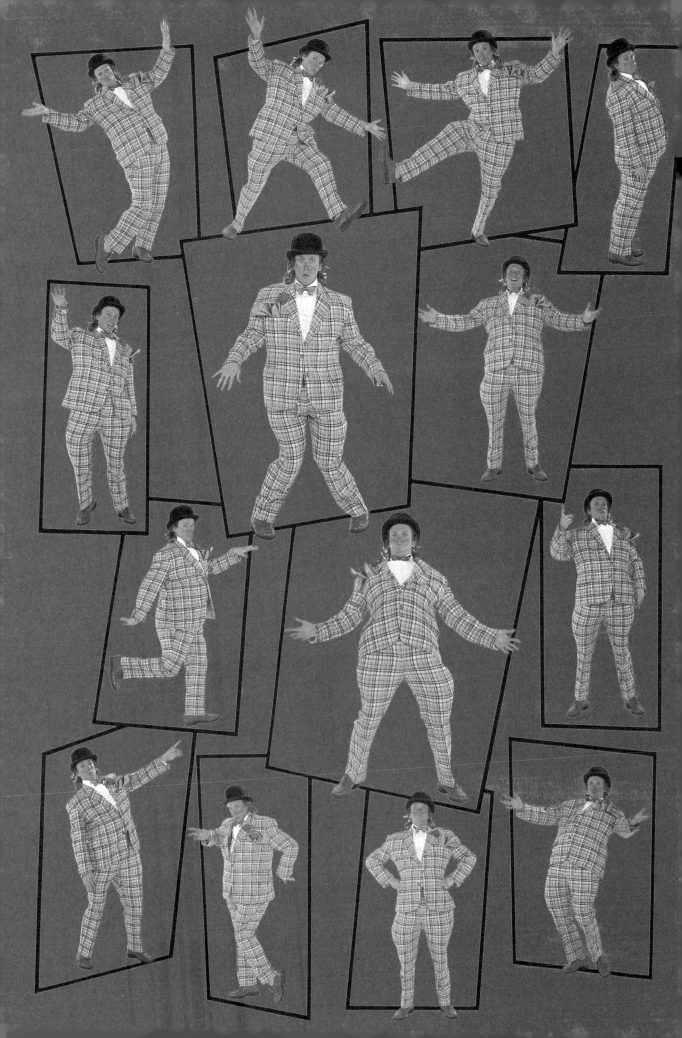